"As our society moves rapidly into its 'senior days,' this engaging, essential book puts a human face on the healthcare challenges of our aging population."

Ken Dychtwald, Ph.D., author of The Power Years: A User's Guide to the Rest of Your Life

"This vitally important book should be read by every single baby boomer—and by their children as well. It's a wise, sometimes scary, and ultimately practical look at what many of us will have to deal with in our lives, and in the lives of those we love."

Tess Gerritsen, NYT bestselling author of The Bone Garden

"The most powerful tool for alleviating suffering is not a pill or an operation. I believe in the healing power of a shared story. This delightful collection of stories reminds caregivers that *you are not alone.*"

Vicki Rackner, M.D., founder and president of Medical Bridges, www.MedicalBridges.com

"A teacher as well as a storyteller, Nicol mines each caregiving experience for the lessons learned while on the job. It's hard to imagine a caregiver who would not appreciate this book."

Mel Walsh, gerontologist and author of Hot Granny

"These heartwarming stories will have you laughing one minute and reaching for a tissue the next. Plus, the tips, resources and creative advice will help caregivers cope and triumph at the hardest time of their lives!"

Jacqueline Marcell, author of Elder Ra~ Caregiving" radio show

SENIOR DAYS

Insightful Tales and No-Nonsense Help
from the Frontlines of Eldercare

COLLEEN NICOL
with BRIAN NICOL

Omaha, Nebraska

Author Colleen Nicol has obtained permission from the clients she served (or their families) to share their stories, or she has used client pseudonyms and changed other identifying client information.

A portion of the proceeds from the sale of this book will be donated to Alzheimer's research.

Library of Congress Control Number: 2007937744
ISBN-10: 0-9794896-0-1
ISBN-13: 978-0-9794896-0-0

Cataloging in Publication Data on file with Publisher

Cover and Interior Design: TLC Graphics, *www.TLCGraphics.com*
Editorial Services: Sandra Wendel, Write On, Inc.
Marketing and Publicity: Concierge Marketing Inc.
Illustrations: Daniel Nicol

LONG LAKE PRESS
A Division of Nicol Ink
13518 L Street
Omaha, NE 68137

Printed in the United States of America.

10   9   8   7   6   5   4   3   2   1

To our parents:

Bev Nicol and, in memoriam, Ken Nicol,
Bob Meneely and Mary Meneely

SENIOR DAYS

*Insightful Tales and No-Nonsense Help
from the Frontlines of Eldercare*

Contents

Acknowledgments

At the top of my list is my husband, Brian, a career magazine editor and publisher. He took my rough drafts and rambling notes and smoothed them into a professional manuscript. He's the writer in the family and my indispensable partner on this project.

Our son Daniel is the illustrator. His drawings grace the chapters.

Many of our other relatives, including our other son Kevin served as sounding boards as we developed the chapters and discussed the artwork. Longtime friends also gave us helpful feedback and ongoing encouragement.

Our publishing partners, Sandra Wendel and Lisa Pelto of Concierge Marketing, gave us professional input and steadfast encouragement at every step along the way. Sandy's editing skills and knowledge of caregiving resources gave the book the heft it needed. Lisa handled the maze of publishing details, from paper and printing to design and marketing. She was instrumental in arranging interviews, garnering publicity and keeping us moving when we wanted to rest. Our partnership with Lisa has become a friendship.

Harriet Johnson, a current client, graciously agreed to write the book's Foreword, basing it on her unique experiences as both a caregiver and a care receiver.

Most important, I want to express my heartfelt thanks to all of the people I've had the privilege to serve during my 13 years as a home companion caregiver. Some of them have passed away, of course; many of them still fight the good fight, with optimism and energy. Each of them—with their experiences, their humor and their courage—gave more to me than I gave to them.

Foreword

I have experienced the eldercare life from both sides. I've been a caregiver and a care receiver. In 1984, I retired from my college administration job at Metropolitan State College of Denver to move home to take care of my ailing father and mother. Today, at age 82, I am one of author Colleen Nicol's senior clients. The challenges I faced back then with my parents gave me valuable insights and a deep appreciation for the service Colleen and her colleagues provide.

When Dad, my mother's soul mate, died, she deteriorated steadily, both mentally and physically. I took care of Mother in our family home, the same house where I live today. She needed me 'round the clock, every day. She was in a wheel chair, and I remember one night she couldn't sleep and she wanted so badly to go for a ride or at least have some physical movement. So I pushed her back and forth through the dining room and into the living room. Back and forth, back and forth, at 2 in the morning.

In those days, there were no Colleen Nicols to come in for a day or a couple of hours to help me out. I do remember our family doctor sent a nurse over every day for a few weeks when he sensed I was at the breaking point.

It wasn't all bad, of course. I managed to take Mother on bus trips to shop and to our neighborhood drugstore soda fountain for a chocolate soda, her favorite. We always talked them into an extra scoop of ice cream for her. She was thrilled.

Mother was 98 when she died. When I look back, I sometimes wonder if I could have done a better job with her, but I know in my heart I did my best. I also know that it would have been much easier with Colleen around.

I first needed an in-home caregiver myself about eight years ago, when I fell during a walk around the block and cracked my knee and broke my baby finger. My sister and I found the senior care company Colleen works for in the Yellow Pages, and I've been using them and their services ever since, even though my breaks have long since healed. A caregiver is with me for a few hours every Monday, Wednesday and Friday. They help with some of the cooking and light housekeeping. They take me shopping, to doctor appointments, to my rehab sessions, to the bank and to the pharmacy. I don't know what I'd ever do without them. For starters, I've never driven, so I'd have to call cabs or take a bus.

I have my favorites, of course. Peggy has been with me almost since the beginning. She's my regular Wednesday and Friday caregiver; Colleen is Mondays.

When I saw Colleen walking up to my door on her first day with me a few years back, I knew this was going to be someone I'd like. And she was. She's a natural caregiver—she's always upbeat and cheerful. She never talks down to you; she never gets frustrated. And just like me, she loves to talk and listen. Sometimes we even talk on and on at the same time. Also, she knows where the thrift shops are in this town. I love to go browse the thrifts, and Colleen has found some amazing ones. She seems to sense what her clients like to do, and she enthusiastically makes it happen.

You'll understand what I mean about Colleen as you read her book. You'll get a sense of her personality, her dedication and her sense of humor. You'll also learn a lot about the caregiving help that is available; she tells you how to find it.

I'm very proud of Colleen and am so flattered to add a few words to her book. I look forward to our weekly time together. She is much more than a caregiver; she's a dear friend. Mother and Dad would have loved her.

—*Harriet Johnson*

Introduction

Grow old along with me!
The best is yet to be.

Not always. For most of us, that famous line from poet Robert Browning describes a hope, an ideal. The reality, as we all know, is that old age can sometimes bring with it deterioration of both body and mind, and oftentimes loneliness and sadness.

As a baby boomer, I notice my wrinkles, fight off my pounds and fill my prescriptions. Knock on wood, my health is holding. But I know that's only temporary and—because of my life's work—I have a pretty good idea what to expect in the years ahead. And, of course, I won't be alone.

The demographics and trend lines of our population underscore one simple fact: Our society is aging. Medical breakthroughs keep bodies and minds healthy longer; the baby boom bulge ensures there will be more elderly bodies and minds than ever before. And already the boomers are glimpsing their own futures, as they devote so much time and resources to caring for their elderly parents.

From the U.S. Census Bureau and the National Alliance for Caregiving:

+ An estimated 35.6 million people in the U.S.—about 12 percent of the population—are 65 or older.

+ By 2011, the baby boomers themselves will begin to turn 65, and by 2030 one in five people in the U.S. will be 65 or older. That will be approximately 72 million people.

+ More than one-third of Americans older than 65 will spend time in a nursing home.

+ Currently, 21 percent of Americans give unpaid care to a relative or friend; 75 percent of them are women, and two-thirds have outside jobs.

Every seven seconds for the next 19 years, a baby boomer turns 60. We're sandwiched, caring for our aging parents if we still have them, and caring for our children who seem to be hanging around the house longer than any of us ever did. As much as we think we're going to live longer and more independently than our parents—most likely true—we will need care at some point. What lessons can be learned about caregiving? As caregivers, our generation will reinvent care receiving, just as we reinvented everything else on our march through life.

The facts and figures seem to point to a future American society flush with assisted living facilities and nursing homes. And not surprisingly, the eldercare industry is thriving. But here's another statistic, from a 2003 study: More than 83 percent of seniors surveyed say they are very or somewhat likely to remain in their homes rather than move to a care facility.

None of us wants to go into a care facility and none of us plans to—assuming we'll have the choice.

There is a choice between independently living in our own homes and the dreaded nursing home. It's an in-between option for seniors that bridges the gap from full health and independence to the need for an assisted living or nursing facility. It's what I do. I provide in-home, non-medical eldercare and companionship. I work for a Nebraska agency that contracts with seniors and/or their family members to provide the help needed to allow seniors to stay at home, the place they want to be. I've been with the company for more than a decade; in fact, I was one of the first caregivers it hired.

I've written this book to share some of my amazing moments with some incredible people. My work has been so fulfilling and satisfying because I've had a wealth of experiences doing what I do. And in a way, it's what I've always done.

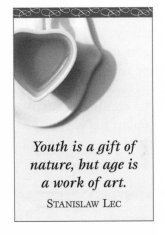

Youth is a gift of nature, but age is a work of art.

STANISLAW LEC

Even as a kid, I loved the elderly. I love their stories; I love their openness and their warmth. When I was growing up in south Minneapolis, I loved the tiny, frail lady two houses away from us. I was 6 or 7; she was 96. I'd sit on her lap in her front-porch rocking chair, listening to her tales, looking at her old photographs. Her name was Mrs. Painter—I never did know her first name, but little kids didn't need to know adults' first names back then. Mrs. Painter had a reclusive, troubled son who lived with her, so I never went inside her mostly dark house. Just the porch. Rocking, talking. When it was time for Mrs. Painter to take her afternoon nap, I'd leave and catch up with the rest of the kids. But I'd be back the next day.

My very favorite older person was my Grandma Meneely, my dad's mother. She was soft and warm, yet protecting and strong. She was in the real estate trade most of her adult life. She and my grandpa bought, lived in, then re-sold old homes and even an occasional mansion. Each of these became a fantastic, mysterious playhouse for my eight brothers and sisters and me. We had amazing Norman Rockwell-like holiday feasts and parties in those huge dining rooms and aromatic kitchens.

Then they bought the farm—literally. Their plan was to quickly turn the spread over at a profit, of course, but it became such a wonderful family gathering place that they held on to it for decades. We played in the barn, cared for the animals and hunted in the fields and surrounding woods. I was still going there when I was in my late teens and even brought my future husband along one time for a fall frolic at the farm.

But about that time my grandma got sick—very sick. Amyotrophic Lateral Sclerosis, Lou Gehrig's disease. She had the "galloping," fast-progressing strain of ALS and was soon in a Minneapolis nursing home, the same one where I had worked in my early teens. She and grandpa chose that facility because I had always spoken so highly of it.

Before long she went from the home to the hospital, as her muscles continued to fail. Her mind was still in there, still strong, but she couldn't move or even talk. The last word I was ever able to understand was a one-syllable request: "Ice." I slipped some ice chips between her dry lips—something simple for one who had done so much for me.

Old age is no place for sissies.

BETTE DAVIS

Later in life, I had another favorite: my father-in-law, Ken. By the early 1990s, Alzheimer's—the Long Goodbye—was slowly stealing him away from us. For the 25 years before that, he and my mother-in-law, Bev, were among our greatest friends. I always said and still say I have the in-laws from heaven.

My husband and I lived in Hawaii for 16 years; both of our boys were born there. Ken and Bev came out to visit us nearly every winter, usually for two months at a time. We'd rent a Waikiki condo for them, and the four of us (sometimes six or eight, if we were toting the boys or if my parents were in town, too) would experience the life and good times of Honolulu.

The telltale signs of Alzheimer's began to appear after the Hawaii days, when we had moved back to the Mainland, to Omaha. On visits to Ken and Bev in Minneapolis, we'd sometimes see Ken confused, forgetful—but always scrambling to cover for it, to make light of it.

Then there were the looks of panic when the mind wouldn't respond, the flashes of anger over something small and, sadly, the vacant gaze where there once had been a broad smile and a quick laugh.

Like so many spouses of Alzheimer's sufferers, Bev tried to handle it herself, to spare us the reality and pain. But eventually we all had to come to terms with it.

> *There are only four kinds of people in the world: those who have been caregivers; those who are currently caregivers; those who will be caregivers; those who will need caregivers.*
>
> ROSALYNN CARTER

I always tried to sit next to Ken at family gatherings. I'd put my arm around his shoulders or put my hand on his hand, giving him a little comfort and security as his mind raced, searching for moorings it would never find.

The care became too much for Bev, and my brother-in-law Larry and his family volunteered to share their home with her and Ken. That worked for a while, with Larry, his wife and two daughters giving crucial, courageous assistance whenever needed.

But the progression was inevitable, and after a couple of years we moved Ken into the Alzheimer's wing of a medical center. We drove up from Omaha three or four times a year to visit him and give any aid we could to my mother-in-law. It was frustrating for me during these final few years—I was working with seniors in Omaha, several of them with Alzheimer's, yet I was rarely present to help with my beloved Ken.

The last time I saw him was at the nursing home. I helped feed him lunch. He gave my hand a tender squeeze, and I think he even winked at me. Maybe, just for an instant, he remembered.

The night he was dying, we got the call and raced up from Omaha to be at his bedside. We missed, by about 20 minutes.

The stories that follow are brief snapshots of special people, people I have worked with in my years as a senior caregiver. Yet, the book is more than a series of engaging tales. At the close of each chapter I offer "Caring Comments," a few pertinent tips, lessons learned and helpful sources. Some of these tips are for professional caregivers; others are for family caregivers. Most are for both. In addition, I've included a resource guide to key organizations, associations and government agencies—all of them dedicated to the art and science of senior caregiving.

Although I was the paid, in-home caregiver for each of the people profiled in these pages, I often felt as if I got more than I gave. They taught me much about life, death, love and laughter.

I hope these tales serve as a reminder that seniors—even when their health is under considerable stress—are warm, compassionate, funny, brave, foolish, obnoxious and selfish. They're *human*.

And we'll be them, someday soon.

I Knew You'd
Be an Idiot

M ary would sit and watch TV but become extremely anxious, even during a simple sitcom or inane talk show. She couldn't follow what was going on, even with the picture clear and the sound turned up. She was lost and confused. Only when the closed captions appeared across the screen could she relax, read along and enjoy the show.

During a conversation, her private, internal thoughts often popped to the surface as talk-out-loud comments. What was on her mind came out of her mouth. Her listener might be mortified or shocked by what she said, but Mary never noticed. To her, it was all just talk—and she loved to talk.

I was briefed about all this—these unusual effects of an unusual stroke—by my agency and by Mary's husband and daughter. I arrived a little early for my first day with Mary, and Bud, her husband of 52 years, was at the door to greet me. He had to get to the library, he said, so before I knew it Mary and I were alone, in front of the television watching the noon news, with captions barely keeping up with the anchor's happy talk.

She seemed annoyed by my presence. She definitely didn't want any help—didn't need any help. She didn't feel there was anything wrong, and so she certainly didn't want any stranger in her house, doing what she'd done perfectly well for decades. It was her home, after all, and she was the homemaker. This caregiver/companion business was her family's idea—Bud and the children.

And so we watched TV.

Finally—maybe because we were both bored—she relented and asked me to help with a few tasks around the house. I do a little light housekeeping—it's part of the job. But we're primarily senior companions, not a cleaning service.

The kitchen was a greasy mess, with dishes in the sink from a few days back. I did them quickly, then went on to some simple vacuuming and dusting. After that, I hauled her bedding down to the basement and put it in the washing machine. Mary was unable to go up and down the basement stairs because of her condition. When I got back up to the kitchen, Mary was starting to get lunch ready.

Youth is the time of getting, middle age of improving, and old age of spending.

ANNE BRADSTREET

"Can you handle cooking lunch or dinner by yourself?" I asked.

"Yeah, but maybe you can help me," she said. "How about salmon croquettes? Can you make 'em for us?"

"Boy, I'm not sure," I answered. "Is it with mayo and celery, like tuna salad?"

She gave me a slightly disgusted look and said, "You know, I knew you'd be an idiot, but I'd have thought you'd know how to make salmon croquettes."

I was stunned—but for just a few seconds. I laughed and said, "Mary, I guess I'm an idiot, but I'm also a fast learner."

It was the beginning of a beautiful friendship.

Mary became my regular Wednesday gig. Husband Bud would be at the door when I arrived and quickly dash away to the library. I never once saw him carrying any reading material to or from, so I was never clear exactly where he went. He just needed to go.

Bud would dutifully return about 15 minutes before my shift was up. He and I would usually chit chat about the stock market before I said my goodbyes 'til next week.

That was the pattern for the first few weeks: arrive about midday, Bud off to the library, Mary and I watch some TV, talk, have lunch, talk, I do some housekeeping, more talk, more TV, Bud returns. Through it all I learned a little more about her bizarre stroke, her Crohn's disease and her determination to regain her health through an aggressive vitamin regimen. We'd also talk about their seven wonderful children and my two and the crazy world we'd brought them all into. We'd watch (read) TV and laugh at the nonsense and scorn the idiots. A pleasant routine.

But, before long, it became a routine Mary could no longer abide.

She became restless, watched the clock, paced the first-floor rooms. Then one Wednesday I found out why: She wanted to go to the casino. She checked with Bud before he left for his library refuge. He said okay and told me which casino was their favorite, primarily because of the buffet. He agreed to pick her up there later. Her smile lit up the living room. "We're going to visit Dr. Casino," she said.

I'm not much of a gambler. Not on moral grounds, mind you—on boredom grounds. Sitting in a near coma at a slot machine is not my idea of time well spent. Frankly, I'd rather be at the library with Bud.

But there we were, at the quarter slots, the constant bells, chimes and racket making me want to scream. I stood behind and watched as Mary went for the three-quarter maximum bet every time. A security guard came by and asked me to either play or move on. I was making other players nervous. Nervous? How can zombies be nervous?

I sat down at a nearby machine and slowly slipped in the one-dollar bills and pushed the play button (nobody pulls that bandit's one arm anymore) until $20 had slipped away.

The next Wednesday we began the routine we would maintain every week from then on: Send Bud off to the library, hurry with housework and lunch, then head for our appointment with Dr. Casino.

When I stood around watching again that second time, she handed me $20 to sit and play. I did, slowly. But then three 7's came up and I was a winner. Mary hurried over to see. "You *are* an idiot!" she shouted. "You never play one quarter at a time! Play all three! Go for the real money!"

She shook her head and returned to her machine. I pushed the payout button and received my paltry reward.

Mary seemed to hit that real money frequently over the next few weeks, often accumulating up to $600 or $700 credit. I always tried

to convince her to quit while she was ahead. Or at least pocket the $100 she started out with. But she loved the game and seemed determined to put every quarter and more back into that machine.

Thankfully, Bud picked her up at the end of our casino sessions and I could go directly home. But come the next Wednesday, before he left for the library, he'd point out that she had lost her $100 again last week. As time went on, Bud's comments about the losses became edgier.

Then one Wednesday he met me at the door on his way out and said bluntly, "Don't take her to the casino."

But inside the house, it was business as usual: hurry, eat fast, clean quickly. Time to go.

I tried to go slow, stalling, hoping it would be too late to take the casino drive. But my tactics did nothing but upset her. I finally had to tell her: Bud said no more.

Well, she flipped, telling me exactly what she thought about me (naturally) and how I had betrayed our friendship and trust. She yelled horrible things about Bud and his stock market gambling. "It's my money and I can do any damn thing I want with it!"

I relented. I wrote a note to Bud for her to sign—"I'm at the casino. Pick me up at 4"—and hoped he'd understand my predicament.

He didn't. He picked her up at 4, nodded a curt hello to me and I went home. And I never saw either of them again. Bud was so upset he called my agency and canceled the home care service. He fired me. I was now Mary and Bud's *ex*ployee.

Like I said, I'm not a gambler, but I'll bet Bud never told her the reason why I wasn't around anymore.

I'll never know, of course, but I wonder if she ever got back to the slot machines, back to Dr. Casino. And if so, did she ever come home with her original $100? I wonder if Bud had to give up the library and stay home with her on Wednesdays. I wonder who did the wash and the dishes.

And, if she has moved on to the big casino in the sky, I wonder if she asked St. Peter if he knew how to make salmon croquettes.

Caring Comments

+ Most people are uncomfortable—even adamantly against—having help come into their homes. Needing a caregiver or companion means they must admit a helplessness they've never experienced before. It means facing the realities of time and aging. Their home was the one place they felt most in control, most secure. Now, even that sanctuary is threatened by the presence of a stranger. Those feelings were certainly there with Mary; she ran a household for 52 years, raising seven kids along the way. Then suddenly I was there. With a little luck and a lot of work, those feelings will gradually ease as the caregiver and the client build a friendship and—most important—a mutual respect.

+ Looking back, I wish I had taken the time to research Mary's medical condition, her stroke. Its symptoms were like nothing I'd ever heard about before, even though there is so much in the media these days about stroke and its signs (which are explained in more depth on p. 44).

+ In addition, Mary was outspoken because of her stroke. It had damaged parts of her brain and made her less inhibited. Imagine what she must have said to Bud at any given time. I did tell my own husband that he had better hope I never have a stroke like Mary's. His answer: "I thought you already had."

Older people often have natural degeneration in certain parts of the brain and not because of a stroke. Frequently it's in the area that controls inhibition. In other words, as this part of their anatomy withers away inside, they become more open, outspoken and can say downright embarrassing things they would never have said in their earlier years. Understand that they are not necessarily being insensitive or rude on purpose if they say cruel things. It just might be part of the aging process.

+ I encouraged Mary to talk to her doctor about all those vitamins, especially because of her Crohn's disease—an inflammatory disease of the bowel. People, especially older patients, don't tell their doctors everything they take. They mistakenly think that vitamins or supplements will do no harm. Sad to say, it's quite the opposite. Many of these people are taking many prescription medications that could interact with each other. Throw in some over-the-counter vitamins or even an aspirin and you might have serious (possibly life-threatening) drug interactions.

+ I still question my decision to accompany her to the casino that last day. Even affected with that unusual stroke, she was a very competent, forceful person. I had to face her wrath when Bud told *me* I couldn't take her to the slots. I caved in to that wrath and made the wrong choice.

+ Now about the gambling. Is gambling a harmless pastime for older people or a problem, just like it can be for others? Opinions are decidedly mixed. Many studies and a good deal of anecdotal evidence point to significant damage—emotionally, physically and financially—to the elderly because of frequent, regular gambling. Other studies, some by major universities and neutral research organizations, claim gambling is no more or less a problem for the elderly than it is for other segments of society. A few researchers even say it is *good* for seniors, keeping them active physically and alert mentally. If gambling is a part of your particular caregiving experience, be cautious and observant. Don't let a pastime become a problem.

+ Kitchen hints. Often the last place that gets attention is the kitchen. I've seen plenty of messy and downright filthy kitchens, refrigerators, ovens and stoves (and let's not even talk about bathrooms). Unless you can afford to bring in regular household cleaning staff, you cannot expect the professional caregiver to do more than light housekeeping because that person is hired to take care of the elderly man or woman, not the house.

In my own idiotic way I assisted Mary with salmon croquettes. Often caregivers find themselves doing more than simply *assisting* in the kitchen. Let me offer a few suggestions:

- Buy easy-to-warm-up foods such as healthy frozen meals and soups. A microwave can be your best friend if mom can pop something in for a few minutes and independently feed herself. It also saves the worry about whether she'll remember to turn off the oven.

- You can assemble meals in smaller portions, freeze them and have a month's worth of meals within a few hours. Some places, such as Super Suppers, can modify their recipes to lower the sodium or carb content to assist people with high blood pressure or diabetes. At the same time, you know your loved one is getting a well-balanced diet.

- Check with your city to see if your loved one qualifies for Meals on Wheels. The free service provides at least one good meal a day, except on weekends.

- Buy food in smaller portioned packaging, if you're doing the shopping.

- Go through the refrigerator and toss out questionable and outdated food items. This is the Depression generation that saved everything, remember!

- Use throwaway plates and storage containers. Keeps the number of dishes to be washed at a minimum.

+ As for Bud, he was a caregiver in need of help. Most family caregivers are. Whether he actually went to the library or elsewhere, he needed to get away to maintain his space. Bringing in a helper like me to give the relatives a respite is something every family should explore. Not everyone can afford a professional, but check into community social services to see what is available and what is affordable. Sometimes an adult day care center can offer a much-needed and well-deserved afternoon of peace and quiet.

Thankfully, there is much help out there. Check the Caring Comments like this at the end of each chapter or the Caring Resources section at the end of the book to find more. Most important, do it now. Waiting to ask for help is the biggest mistake a caregiver can make.

Coping with Caregiver Stress

Caring for another person takes a lot of time, effort and work. Plus, most caregivers juggle it all along with full-time jobs and parenting. In the process, they put their own needs aside. Often it is difficult to look after their own health in terms of exercise, nutrition and doctor's visits. So, caregivers can end up feeling angry, anxious, isolated and sad, and may be at risk for other health issues.

If you have any of the following symptoms, according to the National Women's Health Information Center, caregiving may be putting too much strain on you:

+ Sleeping problems—sleeping too much or too little

+ Change in eating habits—resulting in weight gain or loss

+ Feeling tired or without energy most of the time

+ Loss of interest in activities you used to enjoy such as going out with friends, walking or reading

+ Easily irritated, angered or saddened

+ Frequent headaches, stomach aches or other physical problems

Women caregivers are particularly prone to feeling stressed and overwhelmed. And more than 75 percent of those caregivers are midlife women. Studies show that female caregivers have more emotional and physical health problems, employment-related problems and financial strain than male caregivers, according to the Office on Women's Health. Other research shows that people who care for their spouses are more prone to stresses than those who care for other family members.

On the other hand, caring for another person can also be a positive experience. Caregivers can feel a sense of purpose in their role. They like the idea of making a difference in someone's life.

I care for others because I enjoy the work and make a difference. I can also go home at the end of the day. Many caregivers are often at work 24/7.

You can learn to cope with the stress of this "second" job. The National Women's Health Information Center offers these suggestions at its website: *www.womenshealth.gov*.

+ Find out about community caregiving resources such as respite care.

+ Ask for and accept help.

+ Stay in touch with friends and family. Social activities can help you feel connected and may reduce stress.

+ Find time for exercise most days of the week.

+ Prioritize, make lists and establish a daily routine.

+ Join a support group for people in your situation. Many support groups can be found in the community or on the Internet.

+ See your doctor for a checkup. Talk to him or her about symptoms of depression or sickness you may be having.

+ Try to get enough sleep and rest. Eat a healthy diet rich in fruits, vegetables and whole grains and low in saturated fat.

+ Take one day at a time.

+ If you also work outside the home, consider taking time off from your job. You may be covered under the Federal Family and Medical Leave Act and eligible to take up to 12 weeks of unpaid leave per year to care for relatives.

SALMON
CROQUETTES

INGREDIENTS

1 lg. can salmon

2 eggs beaten

1 cup saltine crackers, crushed

$1/2$ cup milk

Salt and pepper to taste

Celery salt to taste (optional)

$1/2$ chopped onion

+ Mix in order above

+ Make patties and fry in vegetable oil until well-browned on both sides

+ Can also be placed in a bread loaf pan and baked 40 min. at 350 degrees

+ Serve loaf with white sauce with peas

Recipe courtesy of Beverly Nicol

Dog Day and Denny

I never did get the dog's name, but it's a creature I won't soon forget. Mangy, flea-bitten and nearly hairless. Its skin hung on him in folds.

"Don't worry, he won't bite," said Denny, the dog's owner. It was my first day with Denny, but I couldn't take my eyes off the mutt. The dog ignored me as it moved slowly and with considerable effort from one pile of vanilla wafers to another, gobbling each pile down in one noisy, messy CHOMP. Apparently, Denny placed the cookies all around the house, maybe to entice the dog to at least move around a little. I didn't ask.

I did try to engage Denny in conversation, however. He was a polite man, probably in his 70s. He and his flea-infested best friend lived in a dark, cluttered house situated on a hill at the edge of the city.

"Do you have kids?" I asked.

"Yes," he answered.

"Do they live in town?"

"Yes."

"Do you see them often?"

"No."

I felt like an interrogator, so I gave up. Instead, we watched TV. And the sloppy beast slouched over to Denny's chair and proceeded to lie down on—not at—Denny's feet. Denny didn't seem to even notice—another component of their routine, I surmised.

A little daytime program-ming later, I tried again.

"Do you want me to dust or straighten things up, or do any laundry for you?"

"Nope."

"I don't mind."

"I don't need any help."

"Are you hungry? Do you want some lunch?"

"Yes."

"What can I make for you?"

"Oh, you'll find something out there."

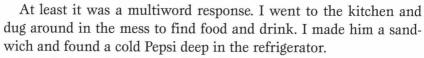

At least it was a multiword response. I went to the kitchen and dug around in the mess to find food and drink. I made him a sand-wich and found a cold Pepsi deep in the refrigerator.

"Pepsi okay with your sandwich?"

"Yes."

He ate, the dog snoozed, immobile on Denny's feet, and I stared at the TV.

When he was finished, I cleared his dishes, cleaned up whatever mess I had made in the kitchen and tried again: "It's a beautiful spring day, how about a little walk around your yard?"

He seemed to brighten: "Okay. Let me get my stuff and show you around."

He started to get up, but the dog wouldn't move. In fact, the mutt seemed to spread himself even more fully across Denny's feet and ankles. Denny struggled to pull one foot out, but again the dog shifted and regained its position. Finally, Denny moved one foot then the other, reacting quicker than the dog. He pushed the animal firmly away and was able to free himself. The dog growled, gave him a look of disdain and slouched over to yet another pile of vanilla wafers.

Denny avoided eye contact with me as he retrieved his keys from a shelf.

"Oh, I guess I don't need these," he said. "We're not going to the store, are we?"

"No, just out in the yard," I answered.

Denny then dug into his pants pocket and pulled out a fat roll of money wrapped in a rubber band. Enough to choke a horse (or maybe a dog).

I had to comment: "Boy, I hope you don't carry that much cash on you all the time."

He stuffed the wad back down into his pocket: "Nobody's gonna take anything from me. They wouldn't dare."

"It's a dangerous world," was all I could think to say, but I knew "they" would dare—particularly from a frail old man. Finally, we made our way outside.

Denny's small house was centered on a prime piece of suburban real estate, a couple of hilltop acres with the ever-expanding city visible to the south. Valuable, to be sure, and with a spectacular view. I expressed my admiration for the spread, and the floodgates opened.

Denny told me the history of the place, how his family came to own it, why it was so very valuable now. He looked me in the eye as he talked; he even laughed a time or two. He was obviously proud of what he had here, proud to be sitting on a gold mine.

He started to get upset as he told me about a certain family member who was trying to work his way into a controlling position for the property. It was that same family member who insisted that Denny needed caregiver help and who had contacted my agency. Needless to say, Denny was wary.

"And I sure don't need any help," he said.

We walked to the edge of the property where his land met a cornfield. He pointed to a nearby subdivision that would be moving ever closer. And he made sure I noticed a nearby lake (a rarity in Nebraska).

He had calmed down and didn't mention that certain family member again as we finished our walkabout. He led me over to his car, a nondescript sedan from the 1980s.

"Do you still drive?" I asked.

"Down to the store and back."

"I sure hope you don't take that roll of cash with you, do you?"

"Yes." The monosyllables had returned. And we returned to the house.

Denny plopped back down into his chair, ready to watch more TV. The beast shuffled over and resumed its controlling position on Denny's feet.

And that's how we spent the rest of our day. Denny and I watching the tube, the sleeping dog in charge.

When it was time for me to go, I told Denny I hoped to see him again but that there was talk at the agency that they'd assign him someone who lived closer.

"That'll be fine," he said. "But I don't need any help."

Later, when I called in my hours, I mentioned the roll of money. I was afraid someone might try to relieve him of it, either down at the store or in the house. After my one and only day with Denny, I couldn't be sure whether he really needed a caregiver or not. But I did know that Denny's nasty, cookie-eating dog would be no help at all.

Caring Comments

+ I definitely had to report the roll of money to my agency. Because memory loss is so prevalent among the elderly, I wasn't sure if Denny would be able to keep track of his cash. I had only known him a few short hours. But I do know that dementia and Alzheimer's sufferers often hide things—especially money and valuables—forget where and assume someone has stolen them. Remember too, members of that "Greatest Generation"—folks in their 70s, 80s and up—have personal or family memories of the Great Depression. They will never completely trust banks and financial institutions. They'll often prefer to keep their cash close at hand, where they can see it and feel it.

+ The immovable dog on the feet was also worrisome. Years before, in a dog-training class with my kids, I had learned that canines are asserting control over their "masters" when they lie unmoving like that. Denny's dog growled when Denny tried to get up. I let my agency know about the dog too, just in case. In fact, "dog dom-inance" is a concern in the world of pet care and training. A dog must learn its place and its role in the household. If not, it will continue to assert itself and assume control until punished or rewarded to stop. Denny had not trained his canine, of course, and maybe it was too late to change things now. The simple beast was rewarded with vanilla wafers for anything he did and had no com-pelling reason to alter his behavior. To him, life with Denny was a good life.

+ Because I knew Denny only a few hours, I didn't see him drive. He was frail; he wore thick glasses. I saw several reasons to be concerned. His family relationships were strained so he may, in fact, have been driving when he shouldn't have been because no one came to take him to the store or out for a meal. Being told you can no longer drive is a traumatic event in most people's lives. You're lucky if they make the decision themselves at the appropriate time. Usually family members must step in and make the call. If a client of mine is driving but should not be, I agonize whether I should tell family members. I always report the sit-

Let us never know what old age is. Let us know the happiness time brings, not count the years.

AUSONIUS

uation to my agency so that they can report to the family, in a more neutral, objective way. (Ironically, I've actually helped five different female clients who had never driven in their lives. So driving was never a concern with them. I think we're long past the generation in which the woman never learned to drive, however.)

+ As the caregiver, you must always be wary of taking sides in family disputes. It's so easy to be drawn in, but rarely will you know the complete story. Worst case, you will become the prize in a tug of war between family members. Watch for the signs of conflict and keep your emotional distance. Refuse to take sides—but do it respectfully and cordially.

In Denny's case, a legal fight over the property certainly seemed to be looming. Elderly legal rights has become a growth industry in itself. Even the best legal minds would be challenged as they wade through the myriad of federal, state and local laws, their requirements and idiosyncrasies. Yet one good starting place for someone like Denny or a family member is *www.legalhotlines.org*, an online, state-by-state listing of legal hotline numbers for seniors.

Should Mom or Dad Hang Up the Car Keys?

For many older Americans, the thought of hanging up the car keys might feel like an end to independence. But you—the son or daughter Mom taught to drive—is now questioning whether she should be driving now at all. Families agonize over the decision, and it isn't easy. In Denny's case, maybe no one would care if he were driving, but at some point, he will come to the attention of law enforcement. Let's hope it's before he endangers his life, your life or mine.

"A senior's driving capability cannot be based solely on their age," said Paula Kartje, an occupational therapy clinical specialist with the University of Michigan Health System. "I have seen some 85-year-olds who have functioned better than 60-year-olds."

But there is no question that the fatality rate per mile driven for older drivers (85 and up) is nine times higher than the rate for drivers aged 25 to 69 years.

Kartje says there are some warning signs that a senior driver might have a problem behind the wheel.

What you observe: dents or scrapes on the car or on the fence, garage, mailbox or curb; seat not adjusted correctly so driver can't see over the steering wheel, mirrors askew.

What you see while riding along: trouble staying in the lane, close calls, slower response, trouble changing lanes or backing up, changing lanes without signaling, going through stop signs or red lights, slow reaction times, problems seeing road signs or traffic signals, going too fast or too slow for safety, problems making turns at intersections and jerky stops or starts.

You might encourage the senior driver to drive only in the daytime, stay off highways and plan around rush-hour traffic.

"Having to intervene with a loved one's driving is a difficult situation for the family," said Kartje. "The ideal situation is that it gets noticed early on and there can begin to be some dialogue about driving, and how they might start to let other people drive them places."

+ *Talk about it:* Sit the person down (don't talk to them about their driving while they are driving) and tell them your concern. Give specific examples about their driving you have noticed.

+ *Encourage the senior to take a driving test or see a specialist:* The specialists can also teach special techniques or suggest special driving equipment.

+ *Help make the transition:* Choose someone who will ride periodically with them and say when it is no longer safe to drive. Figure out alternatives such as a weekly schedule in which family members and friends do the chauffeuring. Post a list of cab services, shuttles and bus routes. Ride with them until they feel comfortable on these alternate forms of transportation.

+ *Have a doctor break the bad news:* You can phone your department of motor vehicles and express your concerns about a problem driver, but a letter from the person's doctor will carry more weight. Enlist the help of a family physician or specialist to break the news. I know someone who called the licensing office about her father-in-law's ability to drive as his license was coming up for renewal (he was 92). They allowed him to attempt (and flunk) the road driving test three times before they took his license away—thus saving face for him, avoiding a family confrontation and giving him a graceful way to give up the keys.

For more help:

Check this online site to start the dialogue: *www.seniordrivers. org* (click Driving Safely, then Quiz).

Use the assessment materials at *www.aarp.org*. The site also lists senior driving classes available throughout the country. AARP can also be contacted at (888) 227-7669.

The American Medical Association includes helpful driving assessment tips and tools on its Web site, *www.ama-assn.org*. The AMA can be contacted at (800) 621-8335.

Sources: University of Michigan Health System, Drive Ability Program; Drivers 55 Plus, Self-Rating Form from the AAA Foundation for Traffic Safety; AARP

The Healing Power of Pets

While Denny's dog didn't seem an ideal companion, pets often are for the elderly. Many nursing homes are including well-trained animals—dogs, cats and sometimes birds—on their "professional" staffs. At best, the animals prove to be good therapy for many patients and at the least a harmless distraction for all.

"At the beginning of life, pets teach a child responsibility and nurturance," said Dr. Marty Becker, a veterinarian on TV's *Good Morning America* and author of *The Healing Power of Pets*. "At the end of life, they provide a way to hold on to those same skills. The senior fussing shamelessly over a pet is a sweet cliché of popular culture ... sickeningly sweet, yes, but also life-enhancing and life-sustaining, as medical and veterinary research increasingly demonstrates in studies of seniors and their pets. Seniors who have pets have far fewer doctor visits than those who don't."

Dr. Becker describes what he calls The Bond between animal and human and its ability to keep seniors active (dogs need walks), to socialize the senior (at least someone is there to talk to, and animals don't talk back), to touch (because touching is something we all need and never get enough of) and to give seniors someone to worry about besides themselves.

Studies have measured the healing power in petting an animal. "Heavy petting" lowers blood pressure, lowers heart rate and lessens stress. Stroking an animal also brings needed exercise for arthritic hands. Studies with Alzheimer's patients have shown remarkable dog interaction with patients who could not or would not speak to humans but had no trouble talking with a golden retriever.

One of the organizations that analyzes the possibilities and power of pet therapy is the Pets for the Elderly Foundation. Its Web site, *www.petsfortheelderly.org*, attempts to bring rejected, abandoned animals into the lives of the elderly, for the benefit of both. The site includes links to many research studies and media articles about pet power. The foundation's phone number is (866) 849-3598.

The Invisible
Woman

I first met Janette at the Arboretum, a seniors-only apartment complex. Her husband had recently died, and apparently she had been showing early signs of dementia. She had a beautiful apartment, and as she took me around, she was charming and gracious. She knew who I was and why I was there.

My first day with her included a visit to the hairdresser, the same one she had been going to for 30 years. The "beauty shop" was located in a private home in a nice neighborhood. Janette gave me perfect directions, but was otherwise quiet during the drive. Once inside the shop, she remained quiet, saying barely a word to the operator and the other customers, women she'd been seeing weekly for decades.

It was a fun group and the conversation was lively as customers came and went during the hour and a half we were there. Janette's beautician was in her 70s and clearly the ringmaster of this beauty shop circus. We all drank coffee, traded stories and shared laughs. Except Janette. She never said a word.

The beautician, very aware of the silent customer in her chair, rolled her eyes in my direction and said, "It's nice of you to bring Janette all the way out here. Do you like your job?"

"I love it," I said. "I get to meet the greatest people."

"Well, Janette has been coming here for years and years," said the beautician. "She gets help from your agency now. We're all just glad she isn't driving anymore. Not that she really did drive much—her husband usually brought her and he'd wait in the car."

She was talking right past Janette, right over her, as if she weren't even in the room. I absolutely hate it when that happens—and it happens often. Well-meaning but careless people talk down to the elderly as if they're 3-year-old children. Or in the case of Janette, because she had become quiet and forgetful and had retreated into herself. It was like she didn't exist.

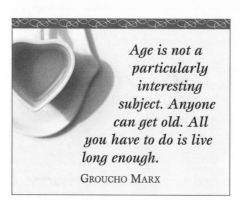

Age is not a particularly interesting subject. Anyone can get old. All you have to do is live long enough.

GROUCHO MARX

After the session at the beauty shop, Janette and I went grocery shopping. She was a little confused about what to get but suddenly remembered she had made up a list and tucked it into her purse. I kept an eye on the purse because I quickly noticed that Janette had a tendency to wander away from her grocery cart and the purse while looking for items in the aisles. Many shoppers are careless like that, but an elderly lady like Janette is easy prey.

After the supermarket we headed for home. I fixed a little lunch for her and asked what she had eaten for breakfast. She told me, and I proceeded to log that information and all of our morning travels into a journal. That information allows the next caregiver assigned to the particular client to quickly and efficiently take over without questions or confusion. It's a simple status report, and it works beautifully.

As we were finishing lunch, Janette's next caregiver, Carol, buzzed the front door and I let her in. Janette silently carried her plate to the kitchen counter. All three of us gathered in the kitchen and Carol, who was Janette's regular helper, asked me if Janette had eaten breakfast.

"Yes," I answered, "she said she had yogurt and cereal."

I had done it! The very thing I hate so much. I was talking past Janette like she wasn't even there. Before I could do anything to undo the way I had answered, Janette blurted out, "I *did* eat yogurt and cereal!"

"I know you did," I said quickly. I could feel my face flush. "I'm just relaying the information to Carol because I wasn't here this morning when you ate breakfast."

It was an uncomfortable, awkward moment.

I still help Janette on occasion. Her family has moved her into an early Alzheimer's care facility, but she continues to get her hair done regularly, same place, same time. The most recent time we were together, we shopped for a skirt and she left her purse in the dressing room when she went out to look for a blouse to try on, too. I quietly  stepped behind the curtain and got her purse and held it for her, while the overly zealous clerk talked to her in loud, simple sentences as if she were a 3-year-old.

Caring Comments

+ Do not talk past or down to someone in your care or any elderly person. Treat them as if they're the age they are—with compassion, interest, patience. They are your parents, aunts, uncles, brothers or sisters. They are you someday.

+ Janette's Alzheimer's was in its early stage, and she still communicated fairly well—when she communicated at all. As the disease inevitably progresses, however, communication becomes more and more difficult, which increases the tension and frustration for both caregiver and loved one.

+ Throughout the struggle to understand and be understood, you must try to be calm, cool and collected. Keep your voice even and soothing, even though inside you may be frustrated and ready to scream. I think I've gotten pretty good at this over the years. I know that my attitude and my demeanor will immediately affect my Alzheimer's client. Remember, that person is churning mentally, on the edge of panic. Don't push him or her over. Instead, provide a safe haven, at least for a little while.

Talking with a Person Who Has Alzheimer's Disease

Trying to communicate with someone like Janette who may have Alzheimer's disease can be a challenge. Both understanding and being understood may be difficult, according to the National Institute on Aging, which offers this advice in its *Caregiver Guide*:

+ Choose simple words and short sentences.

+ Avoid talking to the person like a baby or talking about the person as if he or she weren't there.

+ Minimize distractions and noise—such as the television or radio—to help the person focus on what you are saying.

+ Call the person by name, making sure you have his or her attention before speaking.

+ Allow enough time for a response. Be careful not to interrupt.

+ If the person is struggling to find a word or communicate a thought, gently try to provide the word he or she is looking for.

+ Try to frame questions and instructions in a positive way.

The Twin
Left Behind

From conception, birth and well into old age, they were inseparable, living two lives as if they were one. Yet when the end came, they passed on as individuals, at different places in different years, alone. Lena first, from cancer. Lenore six-and-a-half years later, physically spent, mentally lost.

When I first met them, they were 87. They lived in a simple apartment in a simple building in a less than desirable part of the city. They smiled the same mischievous smile, laughed in the same high-pitched trill and blushed with the same schoolgirl charm. They were tall and thin, almost regal, with short-cropped white hair and lively blue eyes. They dressed similarly, choosing different colors of the same outfit. They finished each other's sentences. They slept in the same double bed. Always had.

They enjoyed telling tales from their fairly ordinary past. One worked for the phone company, the other at an insurance agency for most of their professional careers. When they went out with boys, it was on lots of double dates, of course. They even switched identities a couple of times during evenings out, and their eager escorts were clueless. They sheepishly admitted they'd turned down marriage proposals. "How could one of us be married?" they asked incredulously, as if the question were rhetorical. "We wanted to be sure to stay together. We just plain like each other."

Not all of their stories were fun and innocent. A couple of years earlier they were walking home from the neighborhood convenience mart when a young thug snatched Lena's purse with such violence that he spun her to the sidewalk, breaking her wrist and shoulder. She spent two days in the hospital. Lenore spent those two days at her side. Lena fully recovered, but from then on they took cabs to do their shopping (neither had ever learned to drive) or they just didn't go.

Cancer—colorectal—already had its hold on Lena when I first met the twins. She tried to suffer silently, but the pain caused to her to wince and moan frequently. Lenore would also wince and wring her hands, a glint of panic flickering in her eyes. But through it all she did whatever she could to ease her sister's agony.

The old age of an eagle is better than the youth of a sparrow.

PROVERB

I helped with the laundry and some of the simple cleanup around the apartment, and if Lena felt well enough, I'd drive to the store, the hairdresser or the bank. Sometimes one of my sons and I would take them a warm takeout meal from Boston Market—anything to break their Swanson's TV dinner habit.

As the cancer's grip tightened on Lena, Lenore's panic and confusion grew. She tried to be strong and supportive, but I think she knew she was about to enter free fall. She couldn't concentrate, couldn't remember, couldn't be sure. Through it all she tried gamely to be a comfort and support for her sister. But she couldn't prevent the inevitable.

Lena was hospitalized and died a day later. For the first time in her life, Lenore slept alone.

I spent more and more time with Lenore; she became my primary client. She seemed abandoned in that small, familiar apartment. We'd cry and cry together on the couch where Lena had spent her final weeks. We'd look at pictures, particularly the one of Lena in her coffin, at peace in the beautiful royal blue suit Lenore had chosen.

Lenore asked me about her sister incessantly, and I kept my answers as gentle as possible but always true. She could grasp it, yet it puzzled her; she couldn't make sense of it. She was scared. She'd lost the other half of herself, and now she was slowly losing her mind.

She hid money, she made phone calls, she ordered cabs—but then completely forgot everything about any of it. She'd call me at home to talk and fret as if I were simply in the next room. I'd hang up as soon as I could, but a few seconds later the phone would ring and she'd be back on the line, taking up where she'd left off. Again, I'd try to calm her down and get her to go to sleep. I began checking the caller ID first and made sure my husband and sons checked too. We eventually let the answering machine take some of her calls.

I helped Lenore for more than six years; her nearest relative lived two states away. In my first year with her, I often did her laundry and ironed her many handkerchiefs. Then I'd take her for a ride or to lunch. Gradually, her sadness and confusion about Lena faded into the background.

One day I arrived at her apartment to discover she'd left a pan of water on the stove so long that the water had boiled away and the pan's bottom had nearly melted through.

It was time to make a move.

Mary, the trustee at her bank, and I, along with my agency, made the arrangements for a small apartment in an assisted living facility on the west edge of the city. With the help of a wonderful specialty moving company called Tender Transitions, Lenore and I scaled back two lifetimes of possessions to basic pieces of furniture and several cardboard boxes. Throughout the process, she continued to ask who, when, why. And less often, where is Lena? We'd both cry when I did tell her, again.

Her first night in her new home was not an easy one. She called down to the front desk in a panic to report that her money had been stolen. The staff notified the police and me. My husband and I drove the 10 miles out there and talked to the officers and Lenore. She insisted that her cash—a few hundred dollars—had been taken out of her dresser drawer, maybe by the furniture movers or the maintenance crew. She didn't want to stay in this strange hotel anymore and demanded that we go home.

We calmed her down and helped her methodically search for the money. The police waited patiently. Finally, after about 10 minutes, I picked up her Bible, flipped the pages and there it was, in the middle of the Old Testament. Lenore simply took it from my hand and placed in the dresser drawer, where it should have been all along. It would not be the last time she would misplace money in that small apartment. And it would not be the last time she'd call and report it stolen.

She slowly forgot about that other apartment, the one in the city where she and her sister lived all those years. The nurses and the entertainment director at her new home were terrific and soon were taking special care and notice of Lenore. They made sure she was in the dining room for every meal and included her in the bingo games and sing-a-longs.

I showed up four or five days a week, and the two of us would go to lunch (she preferred McDonald's, where she could never finish her hamburger and fries), to the beauty parlor (she never lost her sense of elegance and style) or for a simple ride (she loved the big houses with the big lawns). We usually ended up back at her building in time for the 3 p.m. bingo game. Somehow, she had never played the game and now she loved it—but only if I placed the chits for her. And only if we didn't sit by "that man who keeps looking at me."

Her dementia marched on.

At Thanksgiving of my third year with Lenore, my husband, one of our sons and I took her to dinner in one of the city's oldest restaurants. She had a wonderful time, dressed so properly for the holiday. She ate a little more than usual and even sipped a glass of wine. The next day she didn't even know it had been Thanksgiving. "It's cold out," she said. "It must be getting toward fall."

Later that year, I took her downtown to see the amazing glasswork artistry of Dale Chihuly. She had never heard of Chihuly but was always up for a new adventure. On our way up the museum steps I tried to explain what she was about to see, but she wasn't getting it.

Once inside the art museum's door, we were immediately beneath a huge, jaw-dropping Chihuly glass creation suspended from the ceiling. The multicolored glass balls, pyramids, rectangles and other odd shapes caught every ray of light, twisted and bent it and sent it shimmering in all directions. We were both stunned. Lenore could only ask, "What is that pretty, pretty light on the ceiling? It's the most beautiful thing I've ever seen."

It got even better as we made our way into the museum to the other Chihuly works. Lenore was so excited she was nearly trembling. Her face was frozen in a smile. "Oh, my gosh!" she said. "The colors!"

At one point a security guard came up to her and told her she couldn't stand so close to the displays. I tried to tell her a little about the artist and his work, but Lenore didn't care about any of that. She said all of the pretty colors reminded her of Easter, when the family would get dressed up for church and her mother had to mark her and Lena so she could tell them apart. She put a red wrist ribbon on Lenore and a purple one on Lena. "The colors told my parents who was who. Sometimes we'd switch the wrist bands to fool them."

Those hours at the museum were the happiest I'd ever seen Lenore. The next day she didn't remember any of it.

About every six months or so, we went to her doctor for her regular check-up, and he marveled at how healthy and fit she was. She was now in her early 90s, but like so many women of her generation, she felt her age was her little secret. Of course I'd filled out many forms for her and knew her exact age, but I never let her know I knew.

The doctor may have marveled at the physical well-being of this 90-something, but mentally the slide continued.

The calls to me at home intensified again, at first a few times a day, then a few times an hour. Sometimes she'd call, ask a question or two, hang up and call back immediately. It was as if she were having a conversation with me and there was no phone or miles between us. It got so bad—20 to 30 calls a day—that we again began checking the caller ID and letting the answering machine do its job.

I learned through the bank trustee that Lenore was also calling long distance to her niece. The niece, in her 70s, had her own health problems, and she was soon pressuring the assisted living facility and the trustee to remove Lenore's phone. I felt little sympathy for the niece, however. According to Lenore, she had never invited the twins to her home for the holidays, nor had she ever visited them at theirs.

I talked to her briefly on the phone when Lena died, and she called the two of them "her crazy old aunts." She sent Lenore a box of candy once a year for her birthday on a standing, scheduled delivery from a local company.

And now she was complaining because of the calls. But the phone stayed. It was Lenore's lifeline.

She and I continued our ritual of daily activities. Every Thursday she'd get her hair done at a local mall salon. I'd shop around while she was in the chair. That was a bad routine for my credit cards, of course. I told her she was costing me a fortune by getting her hair done every week. She got my little joke and we shared a good laugh.

When my family and I returned from a short vacation, I checked in with Lenore and discovered that she'd been hospitalized for shingles. After some routine treatment, she was released. But the pain continued. We tried spinal block pain control through a special clinic. I even took her to a "magnet therapy" session at another clinic.

We returned time and time again to the doctor. The pain was relentless. Yet she was the most gentle, uncomplaining woman I had ever known. Often she was reduced to tears, but nothing could be done. Nothing seemed to work.

She was so confused by it all, she really didn't know what to say or do. Other than continue making phone calls, to me and to the niece—who finally prevailed and Lenore's phone was removed. But no one told me. Had I known, I would have argued with everything I had to let her keep it.

That first phone-less night, isolated without her lifeline, she had a serious panic attack and was taken to the hospital. When I visited her there the next day, she was strapped down to her bed. She smiled at me and started to cry. "Take me home, Lena," she said. "Please, honey."

Instead, she was relocated to the Alzheimer's care unit of a different facility, also in the western part of the city. Here too, the staff was terrific, but Lenore hardly noticed. She was too busy trying to make sense out of it all. Her glasses were taken or lost and the new ones weren't right, so she never bothered. Other patients wandered in and out of her apartment startling her. Whenever possible, I kept her door closed and read inspirational passages from *The Daily Word*.

I took her for rides even as the shingles pain continued. We'd sit and talk like we always did, but she had trouble following anything but the most basic conversations. Occasionally she'd ask where Lena was. When I told her the truth, we'd both cry. When I didn't tell her the truth, she'd nod and smile, relieved. I quit telling her the truth.

One day as I was reading to her from *The Daily Word*, one particular passage reminded me of problems I was having with my teenage sons. The two of them were in trouble at school and home and even with the law. She listened carefully, lovingly, and offered a few kernels of advice (odd, since neither she nor her sister had ever married or had children). My own tale of woe soon had me crying and she followed suit. After a couple of minutes she composed herself, wiped away her tears and sat silently for a couple more minutes. Then she looked at me, smiled and asked pleasantly, "Do you have any children?"

A few weeks later, I returned from another vacation trip and the next day went to check on Lenore. Her room was empty. She had fallen, broken a hip and been moved to a rehab center. I hurried over there. She was in bed, of course, frail, broken, in constant pain. The shingles agony was worse than ever, yet she smiled when she saw me.

I went to see her every day. She wouldn't eat. She was done with food. We'd pray together; we'd cry together. She finally gave up completely. She responded to nothing and no one. The nurse and I would turn her to prevent any bedsores, but she never even winced. She just lay there.

I'd drip water into her mouth and onto her parched, cracked lips. My old Catholic upbringing surfaced, and I'd make the sign of the cross on her forehead just like the priests did when I was a kid. I'd pray, "Please, God, Lenore doesn't want lunch here today; she'd rather have it in heaven with Lena."

She died on a Saturday. I wasn't there.

I picked out her burial clothes—a smart coral-peach suit, trim and professional. My husband and I drove to the small town two hours north of the city, the place her family once called home. The two of us, another longtime friend and a distant cousin's family of three were the only ones at the cemetery, other than the funeral home staff and a local minister. It was a chilly, late fall day and the graveside service was brief.

As we began to drive away, we could see the dark-suited men from the funeral home begin to turn the crank and lower her simple casket into the cold November ground ... next to Lena.

Caring Comments

✦ We all know intuitively that the loss of a twin must be extremely difficult for the surviving sibling. More and more medical and psychological research is taking a look at the phenomenon, especially because there are more twins today, due primarily to the increased use of fertility drugs. For the surviving twin there is counseling and at least one organization, Twinless Twins Support Group. Its Web site, *www.twinlesstwins.org*, includes research, personal stories and resources. The group's phone contact is (888) 205-8962. Here's an example from the Web site concerning the special, intense effects of a twin death:

> "Psychiatrist George Engel 1975, who lost an identical twin in adulthood, identifies three factors that qualitatively separate twin loss from other sibling loss: blurred ego boundaries (including confusion as to who died and who is still alive); loss of identity as being part of a twinship (resulting in decreased pleasure in telling "twin stories"); and a sense of fusion of the self and the twin, which lengthens the time during which the survivor can continue to believe the co-twin is still alive."

Now throw Alzheimer's into the mix, and we get a terrible glimpse at the mental suffering Lenore endured. I moved Lenore from her apartment to assisted living to nursing/Alzheimer's care.

I was with her for five or six hours every day, except on weekends (but sometimes then as well). We knew each other, we liked each other. She had always had a partner, and when Lena died, I filled that role. I became her family. She was scared and lonely. But I'm so very blessed to have been there to help ease the emptiness and possibly take the edge off the fear. Maybe, just maybe, I helped her deal with the loss of Lena. I miss her.

✦ Lenore genuinely enjoyed the colorful glass art of Dale Chihuly. Alzheimer's researchers have become proponents of the therapeutic value of artwork, and more and more museums have added special Alzheimer's/dementia tours to their gallery schedules. Their collections have become powerful means to engage the damaged minds, although nobody is exactly sure how and why it works. But it does work. Said noted neurologist and writer Oliver Sacks in *The New York Times:* "Certainly it's not a visual experience—it's an emotional one. In an informal way, I have often seen quite demented patients recognize and respond vividly to painting and delight in painting at a time when they are scarcely responsive to words and are disoriented and out of it. I think that recognition of visual art can be very deep."

Art—and music—is present, all at once. It's in the here and now. It does not require short-term memory like watching a movie, where someone must know what happened from the beginning to follow the story to its end. Great art touches people deeply, emotionally.

"There's something about paintings and sculpture that helps bring thoughts and feelings to the surface," said Francesca Rosenberg of the Museum of Modern Art in an ABC News report, "then emotions come out."

Art can't cure Alzheimer's, of course, but it can lessen the symptoms, at least for a little while. And that means a smile on the face of an Alzheimer's patient and blessed relief for a burdened caregiver.

✦ Mary, the trustee at Lenore's bank, had been granted fiduciary responsibility for Lenore's financial affairs. Lenore's niece, the closest living relative, also had some say in decisions about and for Lenore. I do not know if the niece had been granted power of attorney rights.

Power of attorney can be a confusing concept, but it also can be very important, especially as the principal (the person authorizing the power) begins to slip mentally and physically. There are several types of powers of attorney, including general, special, health care and durable. Legal counseling is a must, of course. And in this age of Alzheimer's and other diseases of the mind, it's important to note that the principal must be mentally competent when signing a power of attorney document. Otherwise, it is not legally binding. If mental competence is in question, a physician can be asked to certify in writing that the principal understands the document and the consequences of signing it. So the simple message for any of us concerning the necessary assignment of legal powers: Do it now, not later.

✦ Lenore and I spent many hours in her doctor's office. He was her primary physician, of course, and was responsible for the basic diagnosis of both her physical and mental condition. As Alzheimer's becomes a possibility in such a diagnosis, a primary physician will often refer a patient to a physician who specializes in the disease. Referrals may be to specialists in these areas:

  ✦ *Geriatricians*, physicians who care for older adults

  ✦ *Neurologists*, physicians with training in Alzheimer's diagnosis and treatment as well as in other neurological disorders, including dementia, stroke and Parkinson's disease

  ✦ *Psychiatrists*, especially geriatric psychiatrists who treat behavioral symptoms associated with Alzheimer's, including agitation, depression and hallucinations

  ✦ *Clinical Neuropsychologists*, specialists whose detailed evaluations of memory and intellectual capabilities can be key for Alzheimer's diagnosis and treatment options

Even when specialists are part of a patient's medical team, the primary care physician is key. That person has years of experience with the patient and the family and has most likely earned their trust.

+ At the end, Lenore seemed ready to die, her system shutting down, her zest for life vanished. A textbook case perhaps. But our assumptions about death and the elderly often don't match reality. For example, we frequently read and hear that terminal patients go through predictable stages as they approach death. In reality, most will experience anxiety and depression nearing the end, but they do not go through a set series of stages. Another myth: Older men are likely to die at home, older women in hospitals, nursing homes or other institutions. The reality: The large majority of both men and women die in institutional settings.

Whatever the myths and realities of death, the most important, beneficial movement for dealing with life's final chapter is hospice care. And the most comprehensive source for everything hospice related is Hospice Net, *www.hospicenet.org*. Included on the Web site are resources and information for families, patients and caregivers. There's a helpful frequently-asked-questions section to help you learn more about hospice.

Here's how this group defines the hospice concept: "Hospice affirms life and regards dying as a normal process. Hospice neither hastens nor postpones death. Hospice provides personalized services and a caring community so that patients and families can attain the necessary preparation for a death that is satisfactory to them."

Death is the ultimate reality. Hospice care helps us deal with it.

What to do all day?

Finding activities that a person with Alzheimer's can do and is interested in can be a challenge. Building on current skills generally works better than trying to teach something new. The National Institute on Aging's *Caregiver Guide* offers some suggestions:

+ Don't expect too much. Simple activities often are best, especially when utilizing the person's current abilities.

+ Help the person get started on an activity. Break the activity down into small steps and praise the person for each step he or she completes.

+ Watch for signs of agitation or frustration with an activity. Gently help or distract the person to something else.

+ Incorporate activities the person seems to enjoy into your daily routine and try to do them at a similar time each day.

+ Take advantage of adult day services, which provide various activities for the person with Alzheimer's, as well as an opportunity for the caregiver to get a break.

Moving Day

We all hate moving. Invariably it ends up more time-consuming, costly and draining than even our most pessimistic estimates. It's the third most stressful of human events, behind death and divorce. We dread it any time, every time.

Think then what moving is like for the elderly, especially those who are confused and alone. People such as Lenore. When it was her time to move from her apartment to assisted living and later from one care facility to another, an amazing organization of caring professionals was there to help: Tender Transitions.

Founded in 1997 by Sheila and Tom Pettigrew, Tender Transitions steps in to relieve as much of seniors' moving day stress as possible. The Pettigrews and company co-owner Deb Marasco work with family members, care facilities and the seniors themselves to make the inevitable possible.

Moving begins with a plan. "We meet with the senior and family members sometimes a month or two in advance, sometimes only a day or two," says Sheila Pettigrew. The initial visit, consultation and resulting estimate are always free. Moves average about $1,500, although many are below $1,000. Tender Transitions assesses the relocation challenge, lays out a detailed timetable and even creates a "furniture plan" that maps the old space into the new.

The company handles everything: coordinating necessary resources, including a moving company; sorting and labeling possessions; helping decide what goes and what doesn't; overseeing packing by the movers; unpacking and arranging belongings in the new residence; and removing all packing materials and boxes. It's a complete service, with every detail attended to and every special concern acknowledged.

"Most seniors we work with are very stressed by it all," says Sheila. "A few even get sick. This isn't something they want to do." Often, of course, it's the beginning of an uncertain, unsettling stage in their lives. They are leaving their family home and many of their possessions behind, most likely forever.

Sheila shares sad, touching tales about reluctant, resistant seniors and amazing tales about the difficulties of relinquishing possessions. "One woman had 94 slips—I finally just had to count them," says Sheila, "and 150 designer purses."

She also has tales of grateful seniors who graciously made the best of a bad situation and have stayed in touch with Tender Transitions ever since. "Some people even see it all as the next great adventure in their lives, even when they're moving from the family home to an assisted living facility."

Tender Transitions does whatever it can to make moving days as upbeat as possible. The company's three owners and its staff have earned a reputation for being thorough, careful and sensitive. In fact, the company gets most of its business through referrals from past clients and families or from assisted living and care facilities.

Tender Transitions does about 50 or 60 moves a year in its Omaha/Lincoln territory in eastern Nebraska. Its Web site, *www.tendertransitions.net*, nicely details its special moving day services. There are similar senior relocation companies around the country and in Canada. To find one near you, visit the Web site of the National Association of Senior Move Managers, *www.nasmm.com*.

Big Red
'Til the End
... and Beyond

Helena Street and her husband first attended University of Nebraska football games in 1923, when they met on campus and were courting. Eventually they purchased Cornhusker season tickets in the 1960s. The two seats were high up in the north end zone, row 69.

"You could see Wyoming from there," she said later.

Her husband died in 1981, but Helena continued to trudge her way up those 69 rows for every home game, every season, on into the 1990s, by which time she herself was in her 80s. It wasn't really the climb that finally kept her away. It was her incontinence. She'd get up there and be engrossed in the action when suddenly nature would call. Then it was back down and back up, too many times.

"It got to be too much," she said. "My SERENITY suffered because I couldn't DEPEND on my bladder." She'd follow that line with a wink, to make sure her product placement was appreciated.

From then on, she'd sell or give the tickets to friends or family, but she never relinquished possession of them. On Big Red game days she'd plop down in front of the TV or radio and cheer, complain, criticize, second-guess, swear and shout. A typical Husker fanatic.

I met Helena several times in the late 1990s when she'd stop by to see her daughter and family, our next-door neighbors. One day

Helena's daughter asked if I would help out with her mother from time to time, taking her on errands and helping her with simple tasks in her apartment, in a high-rise building only a block away from our house. I quickly said sure, especially because these next-door neighbors had long suffered through the various shenanigans of our two teenage boys, including their incessant skateboarding in the driveway.

I ended up visiting and helping Helena every other Wednesday for the next three years. Sometimes we went to the grocery store or the pharmacy, but mostly we'd sit in the apartment and talk, cups of coffee in hand. She'd regale me with Husker tales, of course, and offer her strategies for making those great Nebraska teams even greater. For example, when the Huskers travel to Boulder for an away game against Colorado, they should go a week earlier and hold their practices there. That way they'd be completely acclimated to the mile-high altitude and wouldn't find themselves dragging by the fourth quarter. It was so simple. She seemed to forget that those players were college students and had classes to attend all week, plus the Huskers won more than they lost in Boulder, despite the altitude.

When she wasn't talking sports, she was talking politics and cracking jokes, sometimes a bit off-color: "I'm busier than a whore on dollar day," she loved to say, even when she wasn't. Yet she always asked about my boys, and, unfortunately, there was much to tell. Both of them were wild teenagers, disruptive at school and in trouble with the law. She often gave me simple, no-nonsense advice; some of it even worked.

This tough-talking 90-something had a delicate soft side as well. In fact, Helena had been the *Omaha World-Herald's* gardening columnist for many years. She and a friend initiated the publicity and fundraising to create a spacious botanical garden in the city. It took years of relentless sweet-talking and arm-twisting, but they got it done. Today there is a plaque honoring Helena Street at the front entrance to Omaha's Lauritzen Gardens, the official name of her botanical dream come true.

She loved playing bridge, and I sometimes helped her plan and cook for her bridge parties. At one session she suddenly announced that she was simply too tired and old to play anymore, and she never did again. Yet she wasn't too tired and old to continue to host meetings of the Lauritzen Gardens board of directors.

My regular, bi-weekly visits fell into a comfortable pattern. The first half hour we'd talk and laugh. Then I'd clean. I'd start in the bedroom so I could strip the sheets off the bed and crack the window open. Her apartment was oppressively hot.

"My daughter says I should take the trash out more often," she said one time. "What do you think?"

I paused for a moment or two. "Well, yes, I think you should," I finally said. "That's one reason why I open the window."

I'd take the sheets and the rest of the laundry down to the building's Laundromat and the trash down to the dumpster. By the time I got back up to her unit, the place was relatively airy. She'd usually greet me with something like, "I guess I'll have a sandwich." But then she'd invariably add, "And shut that damn window!"

The aging process has you firmly in its grasp if you never get the urge to throw a snowball.

DOUG LARSON

So she'd sit with her lunch, watching Perry Mason reruns, while I finished up the cleaning. Then we'd do it all again the next time.

I started to notice signs of slippage, both mentally and physically. Her macular degeneration and glaucoma worsened; she used her eye medications much more frequently. Her incontinence got worse; she visited the bathroom much more frequently. One time I noticed a burned pan on the stove, a sure sign she'd forgotten about a meal being cooked or warmed. When I mentioned it to her, she was mortified and embarrassed.

"I probably shouldn't use the oven with the door open to heat the apartment either," she said.

"Amen," was all I could say.

Her daughter called me at home one afternoon to tell me that Helena had had a stroke. Her worst fear—"I just don't want to be a hulk of a burden to anyone"—was becoming a reality. The family moved her into a nursing home, and I went to visit her soon after. She was struggling hard to talk; the sounds came out an incomprehensible babble. I tried to comfort her by telling her she'd fallen and hit her head and that she'd be back to normal soon. She knew better, of course, and did manage one clearly lucid sentence expressing her embarrassment and frustration: "You know I don't always talk like this." I assured her I certainly did know.

Two days later she passed away peacefully and quietly, as a nursing home aide was reading her that day's newspaper.

My husband and I joined hundreds of others at her visitation. We approached the bier respectfully, but immediately smiled when we saw the large red "N" on the inside of the open casket lid. Helena would be with her beloved Huskers for eternity.

Caring Comments

✦ I hesitated to tell her daughter about the burned pan because Helena was so determined not to be a burden and so determined not to go into a nursing home. But then it became a moot point: She suffered the stroke.

Helena's forgetfulness was dangerous, of course, but it also could have been an early indication of dementia. The Alzheimer's Association offers a mother lode of useful information and resources on its Web site, *www.alz.org*. This simple chart (used with permission) outlines the difference between normal age-related memory changes and Alzheimer's:

Someone with Alzheimer's disease symptoms	Someone with normal age-related memory changes
+ Forgets entire experiences	+ Forgets part of an experience
+ Rarely remembers later	+ Often remembers later
+ Is gradually unable to follow written/spoken directions	+ Is usually able to follow written/spoken directions
+ Is gradually unable to use notes as reminders	+ Is usually able to use notes as reminders
+ Is gradually unable to care for self	+ Is usually able to care for self

My many observations of Helena lead me to believe that her memory problems were age-related, not caused by Alzheimer's disease.

+ There was no question about her stroke, however. Helena suffered a hemorrhagic stroke that covered most of the left side of her brain. A stroke occurs when a blood vessel carrying oxygen and nutrients to the brain is either blocked by a clot or bursts. The affected part of the brain can't get the blood (oxygen) it needs, so it starts to die. Unfortunately, Helena was alone when it happened to her, and there was no family member, friend or caregiver present to get her immediate help.

A stroke is a medical emergency, of course, and every second counts. If only I'd been there when Helena suffered hers, I think I could have made a difference. I would have asked her to *smile*; to *speak a simple sentence*; to *raise both arms*. Someone having a stroke might have a lopsided smile and be unable to speak a simple sentence or raise both arms equally high. One side of the body may show droopiness or weakness. If she had trouble with any one of these, I would have dialed 911 immediately. But I wasn't there. No one was there ...

A Brain Attack—
It's a Lights-and-Siren Emergency

Slurred speech, numbness on one side of the body—even if these symptoms appear and suddenly disappear, they are signs of a stroke and the best course of action is to dial for local emergency services.

Paramedics say a senior will not want to bother them with these symptoms. They think they're fine or that the tingling will go away. But responding to suspected strokes is the paramedics' job, and this is a real emergency.

Sometimes the stroke symptoms go away before paramedics arrive. These small strokes, known as TIAs or transient ischemic attacks, could signal a devastating, life-threatening stroke soon to come. In TIA cases, the paramedics really are glad you called and will insist the senior accompany them in the ambulance to a hospital for evaluation. It could save a life.

If stroke victims can get emergency care within three hours of the start of symptoms, they can often be given medication to unblock the blood vessel in their brain causing the stroke. This type of medication can only be given for certain types of strokes and is only effective within those first three hours.

COPY and POST this on the refrigerator or near the phone, especially for older adults:

Recognize the symptoms of stroke and call 9-1-1

+ *Sudden weakness* or *numbness* of the face, arm or leg on one side of the body

+ *Sudden dimness* or loss of vision, particularly in one eye

+ *Sudden confusion*, or trouble talking or understanding speech

+ *Sudden, severe headache* with no known or apparent cause

+ *Unexplained dizziness*, unsteadiness or sudden falls, especially along with any of the other symptoms.

+ Helena's casket with the prominent Nebraska "N" was a clear indication that somebody—most likely both she and her family—had planned ahead for her viewing and funeral. And that's the way it should be. There is much written these days about pre-planning for funerals and other end-of-life arrangements. Among the issues: cremation or burial, splurge or save on funeral costs, celebrating the life or mourn the loss, etc. Yet those who are conscientious enough to pre-plan their own arrangements often make a very basic mistake: They fail to discuss their decisions and their rationale with family members. Then when the sad day comes, many grieving relatives are surprised by those decisions and may even resist them. Pre-planning should include pre-talking. Get your loved ones in the loop. They might have some great ideas you never even considered.

+ Pre-planning for the end is a much broader topic than casket costs and burial plots, of course. The ugly seven-year dispute over the life and death of comatose Terri Schiavo taught us all how confusing yet crucial end-of-life directives, living wills and other documents can be. Caring Connections, a program of the National Hospice and Palliative Care Organization (NHPCO), has included a comprehensive glossary of end-of-life decision-making terms on its Web site, *www.caringinfo.org*. Here are just a few of the helpful definitions listed:

> *Advance directive:* A general term that describes two kinds of legal documents, living wills and medical powers of attorney. These documents allow a person to give instructions about future medical care should he or she be unable to participate in medical decisions due to serious illness or incapacity. Each state regulates the use of advance directives differently.

> *Best interest:* In the context of refusal of medical treatment or end-of-life court opinions, a standard for making health care decisions based on what others believe to be "best" for a patient by weighing the benefits and the burdens of continuing, withholding or withdrawing treatment.

Do-Not-Resuscitate (DNR) order: A DNR order is a physician's written order instructing health care providers not to attempt cardiopulmonary resuscitation (CPR) in case of cardiac or respiratory arrest. A person with a valid DNR order will not be given CPR under these circumstances. Although the DNR order is written at the request of a person or his or her family, it must be signed by a physician to be valid.

Guardian ad litem: Someone appointed by the court to represent the interests of a minor or incompetent person in a legal proceeding.

Health care agent: The person named in an advance directive or as permitted under state law to make health care decisions on behalf of a person who is no longer able to make medical decisions.

Hospice care: A program model for delivering palliative care (relieving pain and suffering) to individuals who are in the final stages of terminal illness. In addition to providing palliative care and personal support to the patient, hospice includes support for the patient's family while the patient is dying, as well as support to the family during their bereavement.

Living will: A type of advance directive in which an individual documents his or her wishes about medical treatment should he or she be at the end of life and unable to communicate. It may also be called a "directive to physicians," "health care declaration" or "medical directive." The purpose of a living will is to guide family members and doctors in deciding how aggressively to use medical treatments to delay death. (See page 73 for more living will details.)

Medical power of attorney: A document that allows an individual to appoint someone else to make decisions about his or her medical care if he or she is unable to communicate. This type of advance directive may also be called a health care proxy, durable power of attorney for health care or appointment of a health care agent. The person appointed may be called a health care agent, surrogate, attorney-in-fact or proxy.

Non-hospital DNR order: A physician's order that directs emergency medical providers and other health care workers not to attempt CPR for persons being cared for at home. Laws and regulations governing their use vary from state to state.

Palliative care: A comprehensive approach to treating serious illness that focuses on the physical, psychological, spiritual and existential needs of the patient. Its goal is to achieve the best quality of life available to the patient by relieving suffering, by controlling pain and symptoms, and by enabling the patient to achieve maximum functional capacity. Respect for the patient's culture, beliefs and values are an essential component. Palliative care is sometimes called "comfort care" or "hospice type care."

Surrogate decision-making: Surrogate decision-making laws allow an individual or group of individuals (usually family members) to make decisions about medical treatments for a patient who has lost decision-making capacity and did not prepare an advance directive. A majority of states have passed statutes that permit surrogate decision making for patients without advance directives.

A Snail's Pace

Leon had every reason to be slow: five back surgeries, three strokes, left side paralyzed. He was only 70, yet fiercely determined to take care of himself. My job was to make him lunch, make sure he took his meds and get him to appointments on time.

Infirmities aside, I sensed that Leon had always been slow. Everything about him seemed to be geared down, moving at his own personal pace. As a kid, he probably got thrown out easily at first base and was never finished with the test when the nun commanded, "Pencils down!" Laid-back Leon. A lovely man.

He was one of six kids and had six of his own. He was divorced and remarried, but most of his siblings and children lived nearby. He spoke softly and slowly (of course) and laughed easily. He enjoyed discussing his Catholic upbringing and did not enjoy Republicans. His guilty pleasure was those makeover reality shows on the tube—he was amazed and amused by the results.

Yet many times he never even made it into the living room to watch TV during the three hours I stayed with him. He'd just be rising when I arrived (11 a.m.) and he would not let me help him with any of his morning rituals, including getting dressed. He would let me help with shoes and socks, but that was it.

Several times he shuffled into the living room at 2 p.m. and I barely had time to make him a sandwich and make sure he took his meds. I always brought a book along because he didn't even want me to tidy up the house. I probably couldn't have, anyway; the place was piled high with stuff.

My most memorable day with Leon began almost immediately after I showed up to drive him to a doctor's appointment. His alarm clock was buzzing loudly when I entered the house (his wife left the back door unlocked for me when she went off to work). I hurried into the bedroom. The obnoxious, incessant alarm was not eight inches from his head.

I moved slowly toward him, fearing the worst. I felt his forehead—warm, thank God. I tried to turn off the alarm but in the nearly dark bedroom and without my cheater glasses, I couldn't figure the thing out. I jammed it under a pillow and blanket at the foot of the bed. It took me another three or four minutes to wake Leon.

"Oh, Colleen, are you early?" he finally mumbled.

I smiled and said, "No, but you need to step on it; we've got a doctor's appointment in half an hour."

I sat patiently in the living room, paging numbly through magazines while he got ready.

"Colleen, I seem to have gotten myself into a predicament," he said calmly from the bedroom. I asked him to repeat, and then went to see for myself.

A predicament indeed: He had fallen and was wedged between the bed and the wall, his hands gripping the bed tightly to keep from slipping down any farther. To make matters worse, he was naked, wearing only the colostomy bag taped to his side, still connected and full.

I realized I couldn't get in there to pull him up, so I searched the incredibly cluttered bedroom for something to slip under him for temporary support. I tried a chair but it was too tall and too wide.

> *For the unlearned, old age is winter; for the learned it is the season of the harvest.*
> THE TALMUD

"Hang on, Leon," I said, trying not to show my growing panic. "I'll come up with something."

"Don't call the paramedics," he begged. "I'll be okay."

I found a small office chair buried in the dining room clutter and rushed it in to Leon. I managed to squeeze it between the bed and the wall and slide it barely under Leon's bare bottom. He relaxed his vice grip on the bed and slid awkwardly onto the chair.

The office chair had wheels, so I was able to tug then roll him out of the crevasse by pushing the bed away slightly. He huffed and puffed but didn't say anything. Embarrassment was his new predicament.

I got him to the bathroom, found clothes for him and went back to my living room magazines. He proceeded (slowly) to get ready.

We had one more challenge before we drove to the doctor's office: the car. Getting him in and out was very difficult. We decided to take his car because it was larger and he was used to it. But familiarity did little to quicken the pace. He pulled while I pushed. He almost fell on top of me. I almost toppled into the open car door.

Finally he was strapped into the backseat, and I went around and got in to drive. "Maybe next time we should call a handi-van," I puffed. "Please."

We were more than three hours late for the appointment. The receptionist told us they assumed he wasn't coming and had already sent his records back to their primary clinic. But they agreed to squeeze him in anyway.

And so we waited. And waited. Numbly paging through magazines. The nurse came to get Leon and I waited some more.

The checkup itself didn't take too long, and before I knew it, I was helping Leon with his coat and letting him grip my arm for support as we made our way slowly outside—to the car.

I helped Leon for only about three months while my agency arranged for a caregiver who lived closer to Leon's home. After they found someone, I didn't see Leon again. I wish I had. He was a gentle man.

Caring Comments

+ Maybe I should have called the paramedics when Leon was trapped next to the bed. But the tone in Leon's voice told me to keep searching for something to support him. He was sure he could hang on, and I was moving fast. It's those "in-the-moment" decisions that you second guess later. Thank goodness for Leon's determination—and a chair with wheels. If I hadn't been able to get him unwedged, and with no one there to help me, I would definitely have had to call 911 for paramedics to assist.

Leon's cluttered house was clearly not the safest place for a person in his frail condition. But that same house could easily and inexpensively be safer with a few additions and modifications. Home health care Web sites and specialty pharmacies sell a variety of caregiving products including "helping hand" grab bars, fall-prevention alarms and special car door handles.

Here is a simple checklist of ways to make your home safer and more comfortable:

• First of all, I highly recommend a personal emergency response system, or lifeline, in case of falls (See page 54 for more details);

• Install handrails on both sides of all steps;

• Secure area rugs with double-sided tape or non-slip liners;

• Use bright bulbs throughout the home;

- Use plug-in nightlights in areas of night activity;
- Install easier-to-pull handles on doors, drawers and cabinets;
- Install grip bars in tubs, showers and near toilet;
- Place a stool or seat in the tub or shower;
- Use non-slip grip mats for the tub or shower;
- A bench near entrances for setting down purchases and resting is very helpful;
- Install closet lights, plug-in or battery touch.

+ Leon's family should have made arrangements for a handi-van. The vans are the perfect solution for a situation like this. A variety of transportation services are available in virtually every community, including those offered by municipalities, health and human services departments, adult day service providers (home care agencies such as the one I work for) and private taxi/livery services. There are even organizations of volunteer drivers, waiting for a call, ready to get behind the wheel to help. They might not be able to get Leon to his destination on time, but they'd certainly get him there safely.

+ When I approached Leon's bed cautiously that morning and dealt with his alarm, I was afraid he might be dead. What would I have done, if he were? Immediately call 911, and then do everything in my power to resuscitate him. Every caregiver, whether professional, family or friend, should be trained and comfortable in CPR techniques. Classes are readily available from the American Red Cross, at local community colleges and in workplaces. Sometimes training is free of charge, or never more than a minimal cost. Not knowing what to do could have a steep price tag. CPR training now also includes training in using AEDs, automated external defibrillators (the charged paddles you see on TV hospital shows) to jumpstart a quivering heart. These devices are now installed in most public places, are easy to operate and can be life saving. Don't worry, the device won't let you shock someone unless it first determines that a shock is needed.

Police cars in many cities are AED equipped too. Just one more reason why 911 can be your lifeline.

+ What if I hadn't been there the day Leon was trapped between the bed and the wall? An emergency response system (ERS), sometimes called a personal emergency response system (PERS), would have saved the day, and Leon. These radio frequency transmitters are worn by the elderly as a necklace or bracelet or attached to a belt. When there's an emergency, the person presses a button to signal for help. The emergency signal is broadcast to a hospital, police station, physician, fire department or monitoring agency, depending on the particular system. The signal sends pre-registered information about the senior, including address, telephone number, medications, conditions and ailments.

There are several emergency response systems on the market, and prices and fee schedules vary. Most health insurance policies, including Medicare, do not cover the cost. Check with your insurance coverage before shopping for a system.

Also, LifeCare, Inc., a privately owned employee benefit organization, recommends you ask any seller of the systems these important questions:

- Who receives the call when the emergency button is pressed?
- What action is taken once the receiver is notified of an emergency?
- How much is the up-front fee? How much is the monthly service fee?
- How much will it cost to replace the unit if it breaks?
- Is the unit waterproof?
- Are there any fees charged if an emergency call is accidentally triggered?
- How difficult is the system to use?

In addition, LifeCare recommends you get a demonstration of any device you're thinking of purchasing. When buying a system for a loved one, show him or her how to use it and periodically practice using the system together. Emergency response systems aren't ideal for everyone, so check with your doctor before purchasing one.

Too Far Gone

I walked close behind Betty, down the long hallway at the assisted living center, fearful that she would once again become lost and confused. She walked purposefully, her hugely overloaded purse slung over her shoulder causing her to lean a bit to the left.

When she slowed abruptly, I almost banged into her. She spun on her heel, looked me in the eye and snarled, "If you don't quit following me, I'm gonna knock your block off!"

It was my job to follow her, of course. She had moved into this assisted living facility a few days earlier, but from the first moments I worked with her, I knew she didn't belong. Her dementia (or Alzheimer's) was too advanced for an institution like this that provided minimal nursing help and assumed a significant degree of independence for its residents.

As I asked questions of the facility staff and my own agency, I began to get the picture. And it was not a pretty one. Betty had already been "kicked out" of two other care facilities because she was extremely disruptive. This current one insisted they could handle her. They claimed they were confident they could get her to assimilate, to go with the flow, to blend in with those around her.

They also insisted they would not be successful if outsiders kept interfering and challenging them. In fact, they had ordered Betty's daughter to stay away for at least the first month; the daughter was deemed "too protective."

Yet Betty needed protection—and lots of assistance. One floor nurse I went to was sympathetic, but her solution more often than not was based on medication. "That nurse has chemicals that can help me," Betty would declare in her more lucid moments. Because the nurse couldn't hand out drugs indiscriminately, she'd often duck into a doorway when she saw the two of us coming her way. Without the drug solution, she wanted nothing to do with Betty.

She wasn't the only one on the staff who tried to ignore their "Betty problem." When I expressed some of my concerns to the front desk receptionist, she said, "Oh, don't worry about Betty. She's in her own little world and doesn't know what's going on anyway."

The director of the facility would advise me to "redirect her, just redirect her."

Betty was lost, panicky, enraged, paranoid—yet forced to try to participate and function just like any other resident. I'd watch from the hallway as Betty ambled to a seat in the dining room (I'd been ordered by facility personnel to steer clear and let things evolve). Soon she was spilling drinks, knocking food on the floor, arguing and yelling. The other residents quickly moved away from her, leaving her to "her own little world."

To be fair, I don't think the staff was malicious or even insensitive. They simply didn't know what they were dealing with. But to be cynical, I also feel the facility higher-ups accepted Betty when they knew they shouldn't, hoping to get several months' income from Betty's family before "kicking her out" as others had done before them.

One afternoon Betty and I spent an hour or so looking at her family photos—poses and candid shots of people she didn't know anymore and would never know again. Suddenly she began to get agitated and frantic. "The kids!" she cried. "Where are all the kids?!" She had been a career elementary school administrator and now was worried about her many students. Her panic intensified, despite my attempts to console and calm her. She began to sob uncontrollably for the missing kids.

I, too, began to cry—for her, for her kids, for my kids, for all kids. But mostly for her.

Betty suddenly stood straight up, looked down at me and my tears and asked, "Why are you crying?" Her mind had gone off somewhere else, and she was genuinely surprised to see a weeping stranger next to her in her room.

I wiped my tears and said, "I guess I'm not feeling too chipper today. Let's go for a walk."

We did.

I had been a fill-in caregiver the three days I spent with Betty. She was a likable lady in the grip of a relentless, vicious disease. I don't know what happened to her, but even then her fate was sealed.

*Wisdom doesn't
necessarily
come with age.
Sometimes age
just shows up
all by itself.*

Tom Wilson

Caring Comments

+ I have been specially trained by my agency to care for dementia/Alzheimer's patients. They, of course, do not know who I am or how I've been trained, yet I know I can be helpful. I can roll with the punches. I can step aside when appropriate. And I can be reduced to tears. Most important, I can provide relief to the family member or friend who is the 24/7 caregiver. My arrival on the scene allows them to get away for four, six or even eight hours. I'm a lifeline for the family. In many ways, it's the most important thing I do. And I'm honored to do it.

Betty was in the later stages of Alzheimer's, of course, and there has been much written about those stages. Yet when a loved one is in the midst of that desperate swirl, it's difficult to know when one stage ends and the next begins. In fact, there is no straight-line progression. All the stages seem to be there at once. The patient can be nearly comatose one moment and semi-lucid the next. Yet knowing the stages and their tell-tale signs can help caregivers understand better and respond more appropriately.

+ There are an ever-growing number of dementia/Alzheimer's care facilities throughout the world. After all, it's a big business that's poised to get even bigger as the baby boomers age. Family and friends should not cut corners or make quick decisions when seeking the best facility for their troubled loved one. The right place would never keep out family members, as happened to Betty's daughter. Family and facility are in this together; they're not adversaries. If a facility will not let you come during certain times, beware. It is your right and the rights of your loved one to have open access 24/7.

Agencies such as mine send us directly into the home. Home is certainly the preferred choice for as long as possible. When that is no longer feasible, it's time to consider the customary possibilities: independent living, adult day care, continuing care communities, assisted living, full nursing home care (with or without Alzheimer's/dementia capability).

The Strength for Caring Web site, sponsored by Johnson & Johnson, includes a simple chart listing housing options. Click on each option and find an overview and benefits list. Visit *www.strengthforcaring.com*.

There's a growing new option for Alzheimer's/dementia, something in between the usual and customary: Small, licensed houses that offer care for just a few patients at a time, in a home-like setting with first-rate, professional attention. I have volunteered at two such establishments in my city, An Angel's Touch and Betty's House. Both were superb, had an excellent staff with clean, comfortable living conditions.

Barry Reisberg, M.D., clinical director of the New York University School of Medicine's Silberstein Aging and Dementia Research Center, and several colleagues developed the Global Deterioration Scale (GDS) in 1982. The GDS became the basis for characterizing Alzheimer's stages from unimpaired function to very severe cognitive decline. "The Global Deterioration Scale for Assessment of Primary Degenerative Dementia," by Reisberg, B., Ferris, S.H., de Leon, M.J., and Crook, T., was published in the American Journal of Psychiatry, 1982, 139: 1136-1139.

The Alzheimer's Association includes a detailed chart showing the stages on its Web site, www.alz.org. The chart, a modification of the original GDS material, is reproduced below, with permission of Dr. Reisberg. © 1983 by Barry Reisberg, M.D.

The Seven Stages of Alzheimer's

Staging systems provide useful frames of reference for understanding how the disease may unfold and for making future plans. But it is important to note that not everyone will experience the same symptoms or progress at the same rate. People with Alzheimer's live an average of eight years after diagnosis, but may survive anywhere from three to 20 years.

Stage 1
No impairment (normal function)

Unimpaired individuals experience no memory problems and none are evident to a health care professional during a medical interview.

Stage 2
Very mild cognitive decline
(may be normal age-related changes
or earliest signs of Alzheimer's disease)

Individuals may feel as if they have memory lapses, especially in forgetting familiar words or names or the location of keys, eyeglasses or other everyday objects. But these problems are not evident during a medical examination or apparent to friends, family or co-workers.

Stage 3
Mild cognitive decline
Early-stage Alzheimer's can be diagnosed in some,
but not all, individuals with these symptoms

Friends, family or co-workers begin to notice deficiencies. Problems with memory or concentration may be measurable in clinical testing or discernible during a detailed medical interview. Common difficulties include:

+ Word- or name-finding problems noticeable to family or close associates

+ Decreased ability to remember names when introduced to new people

+ Performance issues in social or work settings noticeable to family, friends or co-workers

+ Reading a passage and retaining little material

+ Losing or misplacing a valuable object

+ Decline in ability to plan or organize

Stage 4
Moderate cognitive decline
(Mild or early-stage Alzheimer's disease)

At this stage, a careful medical interview detects clear-cut deficiencies in the following areas:

+ Decreased knowledge of recent occasions or current events

+ Impaired ability to perform challenging mental arithmetic— for example, to count backward from 75 by 7s

+ Decreased capacity to perform complex tasks, such as planning dinner for guests, paying bills and managing finances

+ Reduced memory of personal history
+ The affected individual may seem subdued and withdrawn, especially in socially or mentally challenging situations

Stage 5
Moderately severe cognitive decline
(Moderate or mid-stage Alzheimer's disease)

Major gaps in memory and deficits in cognitive function emerge. Some assistance with day-to-day activities becomes essential. At this stage, individuals may:

+ Be unable during a medical interview to recall such important details as their current address, their telephone number or the name of the college or high school from which they graduated
+ Become confused about where they are or about the date, day of the week or season
+ Have trouble with less challenging mental arithmetic; for example, counting backward from 40 by 4s or from 20 by 2s
+ Need help choosing proper clothing for the season or the occasion
+ Usually retain substantial knowledge about themselves and know their own name and the names of their spouse or children
+ Usually require no assistance with eating or using the toilet

Stage 6
Severe cognitive decline
(Moderately severe or mid-stage Alzheimer's disease)

Memory difficulties continue to worsen, significant personality changes may emerge and affected individuals need extensive help with customary daily activities. At this stage, individuals may:

+ Lose most awareness of recent experiences and events as well as of their surroundings

+ Recollect their personal history imperfectly, although they generally recall their own name

+ Occasionally forget the name of their spouse or primary caregiver but generally can distinguish familiar from unfamiliar faces

+ Need help getting dressed properly; without supervision, may make such errors as putting pajamas over daytime clothes or shoes on wrong feet

+ Experience disruption of their normal sleep/waking cycle

+ Need help with handling details of toileting (flushing toilet, wiping and disposing of tissue properly)

+ Have increasing episodes of urinary or fecal incontinence

+ Experience significant personality changes and behavioral symptoms, including suspiciousness and delusions (for example, believing that their caregiver is an impostor); hallucinations (seeing or hearing things that are not really there); or compulsive, repetitive behaviors such as hand-wringing or tissue shredding

+ Tend to wander and become lost

Stage 7
Very severe cognitive decline
(Severe or late-stage Alzheimer's disease)

This is the final stage of the disease when individuals lose the ability to respond to their environment, the ability to speak and, ultimately, the ability to control movement.

+ Frequently individuals lose their capacity for recognizable speech, although words or phrases may occasionally be uttered

+ Individuals need help with eating and toileting and there is general incontinence of urine

+ Individuals lose the ability to walk without assistance, then the ability to sit without support, the ability to smile, and the ability to hold their head up. Reflexes become abnormal and muscles grow rigid. Swallowing is impaired.

A Gigolo— and Good at It

I t's a formal photo portrait, black and white, probably from the 1930s. It stands among a group of other framed family pictures, on a small end table in the nearly dark foyer. The young man stares from that photo out across the decades, his bright eyes confident and sexy, every hair of his dark, curly mane perfectly in place. He looks a bit like the young Cary Grant or Clark Gable. Irresistible and gorgeous.

Not 20 feet away from that framed photograph, in the kitchen, sits the man himself, Joel White. He's 94 now, the hair thinning and gray, the face lined and unshaven. But the general features and the look in the eyes leave no doubt he's the man in the photo.

Despite the scruffy morning look, he moves with a natural elegance as he works on his breakfast at the tiny table in the center of the room. I have cooked his sausage patties just the way he likes them— burned almost to a crisp. He pours warmed maple syrup over those patties from a sterling silver creamer he says came from "one or the other of my grandmothers." He dips his toast into the syrup as well.

Joel's breakfast outfit accentuates the scruffiness, not the elegance. Pajama bottoms and T-shirt hang from his gaunt, scrawny frame. His worn slippers barely stay on his feet. He mumbles a comment about how he's been reduced to having a lovely lady (me) in his kitchen but being unable to seduce her.

It's the "seduce her" comment that keeps me a little wary, on this my first day with Joel. My agency had warned me that he's a handful: "He asked one of our younger girls to watch a porno movie with him," said the assignment manager. "Now she won't go back there anymore. But we know you can handle him, Colleen."

Yeah, sure.

I take a closer look at the front of Joel's T-shirt: OUTRIGGER CANOE CLUB WATER POLO TEAM. Hawaii. My husband and I lived there 16 years. And in that time we had several dinners and several more drinks at the Outrigger Canoe Club, located at the foot of Diamond Head.

Joel's eyes light up when I mention my Hawaii connection and soon we're talking about a place we both love. He first went to the Islands in the late 1920s on one of the Matson luxury liners. It didn't take long before he was carousing with Duke Kahanamoku and the rest of the surfers and beach boys at Waikiki. The ladies loved him, he claims, and my mind goes immediately to that black and white photo in the hall. "I was a gigolo," he says matter-of-factly. "And I was good at it."

He looks at me for a moment, trying to gauge my reaction. When I say nothing, he continues.

"I'll tell ya, I was sittin' pretty in Hawaii. A woman I met on the *Lurline* paid for everything. From the day I got off the ship until the day I got back on weeks later to head back home."

He begins to sort through pleasant memories of parties and women, mai tais and suntans. How he would meet a lady on the cruise over from California and how she would "take care of him" because he took such good care of her. In fact, virtually everywhere he went, he had a woman footing the bill. To top it off, he had family money of his own. He never worked a day in his life; he never paid any attention to money. Somebody always handled things for him.

But he takes time to listen to some of my stories, too. I tell him about our own fleeting connections to the famous Duke. How my husband's first boss and dear friend lived right next door to Duke's widow, Nadine, at Diamond Head's Black Point; how we once shared a long, lively meal with Duke's brother Sarge at some Waikiki function or another; and how we frequently hung out near the Waikiki Natatorium, the once glorious pool where the Duke set world swimming records in the 1920s.

When people have Hawaii in common, they have an immediate bond. And so it was with Joel and me. The 94-year-old gigolo had become a friend.

My days with Joel soon fell into a comfortable routine. His failing health in general had been exacerbated by a broken hip from a recent fall, so we rarely went out. After the usual breakfast we'd sit in his living room and listen to some of his LPs; he had an amazing collection of records from the 1920s to the 1960s. I'd dig out the album he requested and, careful to hold it gingerly by the edges, place it on the turntable of his vintage German Grundig Majestic. He had an identical phonograph in his bedroom.

We'd listen to Nat King Cole, Cyd Charise, Cole Porter, Montovanni, Frank Sinatra and every musical ever performed. He seemed to slip into a trance while the music played and I nearly did too. I loved it all—well, maybe not Sinatra. "You're a smart one," he commented one day at the end of a session, and I was never sure why he said it. Maybe because if I liked most of the music he liked, I must be smart.

Between albums he'd tell stories from his New York days, his Hollywood days. Every tale centered around a beautiful woman and, of course, the gigolo Joel White. But his stories were never salacious; his conquests almost seemed courtly. It was as if he were spinning yarns about love, not sex. Again, I imagined Cary Grant, Clark Gable.

You know, by the time you reach my age, you've made plenty of mistakes if you've lived your life properly.

RONALD REAGAN

But there was a dark side to the gorgeous young man in the photo, and I started to see it in small ways. I asked him who were the two little girls in one of the other photos in the hall. They are his daughters, he said, and getting old themselves by now. In fact, one of them—I was never sure which—now was making the financial and legal decisions for Joel, and he didn't like it one bit. "She says I don't mean that much to her; I'm nothing but a sperm donor. Well, this sperm donor married her mother and made an honest woman of her."

He told me how he broke his hip. He took a swing at his long-suffering girlfriend, missed and went sprawling. He's still angry, he said. "If the sex with her hadn't been so great, I'd never of stayed with her that long." Sex so great? At 94?

One day after breakfast I helped him into his bedroom, onto the commode next to his bed and then retreated back out through the bedroom to wait in the hall.

"Colleen," he called out after a short time. "I soiled my pajama bottoms. Can you come here and get me some clean ones out of the dresser?"

I went into the bedroom, and saw he was still seated, the pajamas down around his ankles.

"The clean ones are in the bottom drawer," he said. I went to the dresser, pulled open the drawer and saw nothing but PORNOGRAPHY. Movie tapes with the most graphic art on the sleeve casings you could ever imagine, nearly cascading out of the drawer.

"Well, for God's sake!" I slammed the drawer closed. "What the—!"

"Well, you can't blame a guy for tryin'." He sat on that commode, a big smile on his face. At least he didn't ask me to watch one of the movies with him. Figured I was too smart, I guess. Or maybe too old.

Then one day out of the blue I got word he had been moved to Brighton Gardens, an assisted living facility. His daughter and her lawyer had forced the relocation because Joel wasn't paying any of his considerable bills and his house would have to be sold to get him out of debt. He no longer could afford home care service.

Needless to say, he was furious. I visited him at Brighton on my own, and his girlfriend was there. To my absolute surprise, he told her I would be "representing him," and he wanted to give me the key to his house so I could check on it. She talked him out of it, leaving him sulking and refusing to finish his lunch. I wheeled him back to his room.

The girlfriend met me outside and briefly outlined the disarray of Joel's finances. His daughter was selling his house to pay off his debts; locks had already been changed.

Joel continued to run up bills at Brighton and was becoming unruly, often taking his anger out on the staff. He couldn't believe that none of them—nurses, maids, not even the entertainment director—would sit down with him and listen to his record albums. Not only that, the food was "shitty," they wouldn't warm his syrup, he could have only four sausages—link not patty and not burned!

Because I knew staff at Brighton, I was able to get his syrup heated, but he couldn't believe I would just leave him there, "incarcerated by his very own daughter." I didn't have the heart to tell him I'd seen a "for sale" sign in front of his house.

Not long after that, he was transferred to another facility, more of a nursing home than an assisted living residence. I went to see him a couple of times, not for work but just to see how he was doing.

"They sold my goddamned house!" he greeted me on one visit. He sat in the dining room, hunched down in a wheelchair, shrouded in an afghan, skinnier than ever. He was arguing with the wait staff about the sausage, refusing to ever give up the fight.

"And this place stinks!" he added for emphasis.

My last visit there, I helped tuck him into bed for an afternoon nap. His health was deteriorating fast. As I was leaning over to reposition him on the bed, he put his arms around my shoulders and said, "Ah, a lovely lady in my arms. It feels so nice again."

I smiled and whispered, "And you're still good at it."

Caring Comments

+ A reminder, obvious but worth stating: Some folks in their 90s can have intense sexual appetites and desires just like they did in their 20s. Clearly, Joel had lost none of his enthusiasm for members of the opposite sex. My agency had warned me, of course, but the caregiver before me was caught unawares, much to her dismay. Our role is not to judge but make sure the senior in our care is safe.

+ Joel and I formed a bond almost immediately because of that Hawaii connection. Our island memories ensured we always had something to talk about. As a caregiver, give of yourself as you try to draw your client out. Find those common denominators, even if they seem insignificant. You'll be surprised how far they can take you. And if your client suffers from Alzheimer's/dementia, those conversations about mutual experiences, shared likes, dislikes—whatever—will often provide a refuge for both you and your client. You can return to that refuge as often as you please.

+ Unpaid bills can be a sign the senior is slipping. People who never missed a house payment or utility bill can find themselves over-whelmed with piles of unpaid bills and charitable solicitations (that's another story) and unable to figure out their finances. At this point, if all the planning had gone according to schedule, a family member would step in with power of attorney and take over the financial affairs. Sadly, it might be a utility company that alerts a responsible party that bills are unpaid. As difficult as it is for a senior to understand electronic bill paying, these can be safe-guards to literally keeping the "lights on."

+ Because of my fondness for Joel, I almost got caught up in a family dispute that had gotten ugly and litigious. I didn't know what to say or think when he suddenly told his girlfriend I would be "representing" him. He had complained about his daughter, some lawyer, his girlfriend and all "those stupid bills" in his desk. I would have gotten in way too deep had I sided with him in disputes I knew nothing about. When I called my agency to explain what was going on, they advised me in no uncertain terms: Stay out of it.

In a perfect world, Joel and his daughter (and any other family members) would have gotten many of the details of life straight-ened out and agreed upon long before it was time for Joel to move to a nursing home. They would have signed formal documents, filed legal papers, made lists and left a paper trail. The confusion, disagreements and bitterness could have been avoided. Something tells me Joel and his daughters never sat down and drew up that kind of list.

Make Life-or-Death Decisions Now

Only 36 percent of Americans have a living will (also called an advance directive), spelling out whether they want life-sustaining medical care in case they are terminally ill or incapacitated, according to a survey by FindLaw, a leading legal Web site, *www.findlaw.com.*

What is a living will?

A living will is a document in which you can indicate your instructions in advance as to what medical treatments you wish to receive in the event of terminal illness or permanent unconsciousness. Under certain conditions, it permits doctors to withhold or withdraw life support systems. Without a living will, medical care decisions are generally made by your spouse, guardian, health care agent or a majority of parents and children. But if family members and doctors have difficulty deciding on medical care, the matter could be decided in court.

A living will can help you be in charge of your own destiny. You decide. Critical decisions are not left to chance or the unknown.

FindLaw offers the following tips for creating a living will:

+ *Make sure your living will conforms to your state's laws:*
  A living will must meet specific legal requirements.
  For example, some states require it to contain specific language and be signed in the presence of two qualified witnesses as well as certified by a notary public or a clerk of the superior court. Your lawyer can advise you.

+ *Make clear, consistent choices:* To be effective, the document should specify not only whether you want extraordinary life-saving measures, but also whether you wish to receive pain medication, artificial nutrition or hydration.

+ *Store extra copies:* Keep the original in a place where family members can easily find it. If your state law allows, you may wish to sign several copies, have each witnessed and certified, and give an original to the appropriate people, such as family members and family doctors. However, if you change your mind and revoke or change your living will, make sure you destroy all previous originals and copies.

+ *Appoint a health care agent:* You may wish to designate a specific person as your health care agent by signing a health care power of attorney or general durable power of attorney document. The health care agent will then have the authority to carry out your wishes and make decisions regarding your care.

+ *Review your living will if you move:* A living will may not be valid if you move to another state. If you spend a significant amount of time in another state, you may want to sign a living will for each state. However, in some states this may invalidate previously signed living wills.

+ *Consult an estate-planning attorney:* Living wills and powers of attorney may be invalidated or contested if there are errors or problems conforming to state law. You can find a qualified, experienced estate-planning attorney in your area using online lawyer directories such as FindLaw, *http://lawyers.findlaw.com/*.

Second Sight

M arge received the care she needed, and then some. Twice a week a nurse aide arrived at the house and gave her a sponge bath. A volunteer caregiver dusted her living room and bedroom daily, and Marge's daughter Becky scrubbed her bedroom floor once a week. Becky gave up a teaching career to be there constantly for her mother. And then there was me—my job was to spend a few hours with Marge in the middle of the day twice a week so that Becky could run errands, do housework and tend to her own busy life.

Marge certainly needed that care: She was bedridden, with tubes, cables and equipment everywhere. A feeding tube went into her stomach; a trachea allowed her to breathe. She was partially deaf and completely blind—had been for years. Marge probably should have been in a nursing home, but Becky resisted. She wanted her mother at home, "where she belonged," even though the ongoing attention and care was a struggle for Becky, who was quite heavy and not in the best of health herself.

When I sat with Marge, I'd hold her hand and talk loudly. She'd shake her head, laugh and scowl. She seemed to delight in my company, as did I in hers.

Apparently all the loving care, valuable time and significant resources devoted to this long-suffering woman were not enough. Someone complained to Adult Protective Services (APS), and an inspector/case worker showed up one morning unannounced, to investigate the anonymous complaint. I was stunned. Daughter Becky was stunned, hurt and mad.

Over the next few weeks, inspectors made frequent, surprise visits and hit Becky with a continual avalanche of forms to fill out, documents to find and reports to file. When Marge figured out what was going on, she too became very agitated.

A pastor from their church came once a week to give Marge communion. He and his wife were shocked when they heard about the prying, suspicious people from APS. The pastor wanted to set APS straight, but the bureaucrats were not interested in what he had to say.

The APS inspectors found nothing, admitted defeat and apologized to Becky. She simply kept doing what she had been doing all along: caring for and protecting her mother.

Marge's overall condition continued to deteriorate, and I wondered how long Becky could ignore the nursing home reality.

Then one day, another surprise. An amazing one. Becky met me at the door like she always did, but with a wide smile on her face.

"Wait 'til you get a load of this," she said.

I followed her into Marge's room, and she said to her mother, "Mom, look how cute Colleen is."

Marge, too, was smiling. She mouthed and "talked" through the trachea tube: "I love her short hair."

She could see. For the first time in years, there was light in her life. For once in my life I was absolutely speechless.

Becky filled me in: About an hour or so before I arrived, Becky was cleaning and dressing Marge for the day when suddenly her mother said, "I like that blouse."

Incredulous, Becky managed to ask, "What does my blouse look like, Mom?"

"It's striped," answered Marge. "It looks like a circus tent."

Later that morning several friends and relatives came over to witness the miracle, including the pastor and his wife. More than a few tears of joy were shed by all.

Except Marge. She couldn't understand what all the fuss was about. It was as if she didn't realize that she had been blind for years.

Marge's doctor was skeptical but had no explanation.

From then on, my visits with Marge included not only chatting, holding hands and occasional trachea clearing, but also television watching. Her second sight never diminished.

My relationship with Marge ended abruptly, as they often do in my line of work. My agency called to tell me that Marge was no longer a client, so I should terminate my regular visits. I couldn't leave it at that, of course. I left several phone messages for Becky before finally connecting. She didn't want to talk about it, other than to make an angry, weary comment about "Medicare." I called again, to try to find out more, but there was no answer.

I never heard from Becky again; I never saw Marge again (and she never saw me and my short hair). I assume the inevitable became reality: a nursing home.

*Age wrinkles
the body.
Quitting wrinkles
the soul.*

Douglas MacArthur

Caring Comments

+ The inspectors from Adult Protective Services never talked to me, even though I was with Marge and Becky twice a week. They weren't interested in my opinion, I guess. But they should have been. I witnessed Becky's love and devotion. I saw the cleanliness and constant care. And I recognized the fear in Marge's voice when she answered those incessant questions from the inspectors. She knew they were trying to build a case to force her into a nursing home.

Yet I have to look at the bigger picture. APS was simply doing its job, protecting the elderly from neglect or abuse. After all, they had received a tip and were following up, thoroughly and professionally.

The frequency of elder abuse is difficult to measure; as much as 85 percent may go unreported. The Senate Special Committee on Aging estimates there may be as many as 5 million elder abuse victims every year.

What constitutes elder abuse? The National Center on Elder Abuse (NCEA), (202) 898-2586, is the best source for information. The NCEA's Web site, *www.elderabusecenter.org*, defines elder abuse as a term referring to any knowing, intentional or negligent act by a caregiver or any other person that causes harm or a serious risk of harm to a vulnerable adult. The specificity of laws varies from state to state, but broadly defined, abuse may be:

+ *Physical Abuse:* Inflicting, or threatening to inflict, pain or injury on a vulnerable elder, or depriving them of a basic need. If you see bruises or burns, you could be seeing abuse. Unexplained broken bones are another sign.

+ *Emotional Abuse:* Inflicting mental pain, anguish or distress on an elder person through verbal or nonverbal acts. If the senior withdraws from normal activities or seems unusually despondent or depressed, he or she may be under emotional distress from abuse. A family member may be threatening the senior or yelling. Frequent arguments could also indicate emotional stress.

+ *Sexual Abuse:* Non-consensual sexual contact of any kind.

+ *Exploitation:* Illegal taking, misuse or concealment of funds, property or assets of a vulnerable elder. Unexplained withdrawals from the bank, unauthorized use of the ATM and credit cards could all mean someone is exploiting the senior.

+ *Neglect:* Refusal or failure by those responsible to provide food, shelter, health care or protection for a vulnerable elder. Bedsores, poor hygiene may indicate neglect. Weight loss could mean the senior is not getting meals.

+ *Abandonment:* The desertion of a vulnerable elder by anyone who has assumed the responsibility for care or custody of that person.

Becky did confide in me that she had a pretty good idea who had sent the APS people her way. She and I had become close; we both were ready to circle our wagons around her mother. Yet after Becky had canceled my caregiving services, she seemed distant and cold when I called to say goodbye to her mother. Maybe she was embarrassed by the abruptness of it all. But I wanted to make sure Marge knew that short-haired Colleen had sent her love, one last time.

It's a Miracle

Shortly after the DC-10 took off from New York's Kennedy Airport, there was a loud explosion on board. Most of the passengers on the plane were Jews on a pilgrimage to Jerusalem to visit the Wailing Wall and other sites sacred to their faith. Not long after the startling noise, the pilot announced that the flight would continue on to its destination rather than return to New York. The aircraft was fine, he assured everybody.

But a couple of hours out, there was another explosion, this one shaking the plane from nose to tail. The pilot announced that one engine was gone and they'd attempt to make it to Tel Aviv. "But it's going to be very rough," he said, "so seatbelts fastened tightly, please."

The plane jerked and shuddered, rolled and bounced. Passengers were sick, crying, screaming. The pilot came back on the intercom and told everyone to pray. And lo and behold, all of those Jews got down on their knees and prayed to the Lord Jesus. Yes, the very same Jesus that they had murdered two thousand years before. Jesus, the Son of God. The Jews all got down on their knees and accepted Jesus as their Savior.

And the plane landed safely.

The congregation was silent. A few were crying. I sneaked a look at the seemingly normal people around me and was amazed, dumbfounded. They all seemed to have fallen for it, believed that story. Not only that, they seemed moved by it. (An explosion at take-off? Fasten your seatbelts and pray? I'll say! Jewish people kneeling down in a crippled plane? Where, in the aisle? On the seats? With all that leg room? And they accepted Jesus as their Savior?)

Slowly, several members of the congregation rose up out of their chairs and walked respectfully to the front of the church. Others moved in behind them. The preacher stood serenely at the front to greet them, his storytelling over, his collecting now beginning. Each person put money—folding money—into the shiny golden cauldron at the right hand of the preacher.

Libby, sitting on my right, leaned over to me, a $20 bill in her hand, and said, "Here, Honey, you're the only one not giving money. Don't be left out."

The old believe everything; the middle aged suspect everything: the young know everything.

OSCAR WILDE

I held up my hand, rejecting the offer, and whispered, "Thank you, Libby, but I don't even want to give them *your* money."

Her face flushed and she seemed confused. She slid the $20 into the back of her checkbook, quickly wrote out a check and hurried up to join the line. I sat there alone, the only one who hadn't gotten up to give—and proud of myself for not doing so.

Up front the preacher was filling the silence by hammering home his message: "When you accept the Lord Jesus as your Savior, your life only gets better and miracles do happen. But only if you let Jesus into your life! Accept Jesus as your Savior! It's the only way to heaven—as all those Jews now know!"

I watched Libby drop her check in the golden bowl, knowing she wouldn't be mad at me or even disappointed. In fact, she most likely wouldn't remember any of this.

Libby, 87, was in the middle stages of Alzheimer's. Despite her frequent confusion and fear, she still carried herself with style and grace. She was tall and slender, silver haired. It was easy to imagine her a stunning beauty all those decades ago. We had paged through photo albums in her simple home, and I quickly saw she had been a stunning beauty, even in black and white.

For the last two years, she and I had done some of the customary things together: trips to the store, appointments at the hair salon, stops at the bank. But the activity she appreciated most and couldn't get enough of was church. Not just any church, but Salvation's Nest, with its stories of Jewish conversion on planes and angels up for sale. Libby loved that house of worship and its silver-tongued preachers.

They came to town twice a year, three of them, with their wives. They'd drive into the strip mall and park directly in front of the church's nondescript, rented storefront. Their three vehicles were anything but nondescript: a white Excursion, a beige Mercedes and a black Cadillac. All three sported Louisiana license plates.

All three preachers—middle-aged white men—sported slicked-back shiny hair-dos dyed in black, brown, red or combinations thereof. Their suits were never gray flannel conservative. Instead, they came in colors best described as electric blue, emerald green and mustard yellow. One of them sometimes appeared in a unique iridescent gray double-breasted sharkskin ensemble.

Their wives did not pale in comparison: multicolored dresses, amazing high heels, blinding jewelry, too much makeup, too much hair. The second comings of Tammy Faye Bakker.

To my amazement, the churchgoers filing into the building were never put off by the arrival spectacle but, in fact, seemed genuinely impressed. The congregation was a reflection of the community itself: multiethnic, multiclass. They always came prepared to get inspiration and give money.

That was certainly true of Libby. She casually told me one time on our drive to the church that her will had been rewritten to leave significant sums of money to the church's "building fund" and to the three preachers themselves. The news gave me the chills.

I later checked with the bank trustee who was handling Libby's finances. The trustee could not divulge details of the will or any other private information, but later one of Libby's relatives did confirm that dismaying reality: The reverends from Louisiana were entitled and they didn't even know it.

A recently divorced Texas woman who attended a Salvation's Nest meeting hoped to receive some comfort and solace in her difficult time.

She had brought along her three young daughters, each of them blonde and beautiful—"pageant winners."

She had heard she could "buy an angel" at the meeting. The Lord's angels are there to help us when we need them, to be our special protectors when we're in harm's way. But we must earn an angel, and we earn an angel by supporting the church and its mission of goodness and faith.

The Texas woman was barely making ends meet, but she loved our Savior. And she loved her daughters. She agonized as she listened to my sermon and witnessed the rapture on other faces in the crowd after they bought their angels.

The woman made her decision, listened to her heart: She took out her checkbook, wrote a check and walked to the front of the congregation. She put her check into our cauldron; she purchased an angel and felt its warmth envelop her immediately.

Later that night she drove the freeway toward home, her three daughters asleep in the car. Suddenly another vehicle came out of nowhere and crashed into her, sending her car spinning violently. All three daughters were thrown from the vehicle and went tumbling onto the asphalt.

The stunned, panicky mother climbed out from behind the wheel and the discharged airbag and ran back to her blonde darlings. As she quickly went to them one by one, each smiled at her and said, "I'm okay, Mommy." She could hear the sirens wailing in the background.

As the tears streamed down her cheeks, she said to herself, "Thank God I gave $1,000 to buy an angel tonight. We won't be needing that ambulance."

"Now all of you can make your own decisions tonight," continued the preacher in gray sharkskin. "How much should you give to buy an angel? Take out your checkbooks or currency and just remember that blessed lady from Texas and her three beautiful little girls. Give what your heart says you can afford."

The line formed quickly. Libby hesitated. She glanced at me; I stared straight ahead. As the others secured their angel by placing their checks and currency into the cauldron, the preachers placed their hands on their heads in blessing or shook their hands in gratitude. The room echoed with a variety of calls to "Praise the Lord!" Still Libby hesitated.

"I want to buy an angel," she said to me softly. "Do *you*?"

I wanted to scream out "No!" as loud as I could, but instead I took the high road. I smiled and said, "No, thank you, but you go ahead."

Libby got out her checkbook and started to write, turning slightly so I couldn't see the amount. She was clearly uncomfortable.

"I'm going to go in the back for a minute," I said. "You go get your angel."

I slipped away to the rear of the room and Libby finished her check. She then joined the line, deposited her money, was thanked effusively by Reverend Sharkskin and made her way back to her chair.

She glanced at me and smiled. I smiled back, feeling just a little guilty for possibly making *her* feel guilty for doing what she wanted to do. After all, it was her money and now it was her angel. But still …

A few weeks after Angel Night, Libby suffered a severe stroke and died within two days. Nobody from the church was at the funeral; I doubt if any of them even knew.

Her nephew, her closest living relative, called me shortly there-after to thank me for being a helpful companion to his aunt in her final years. We talked about Libby and the fam-ily for a while and then he asked me what I knew about the church and the ministers from Louisiana. I gave him the Cliffs Notes version of the story.

"Well, the family was pretty surprised by the will," he said. "She left that church $100,000 and each of the three ministers $10,000."

I almost dropped the phone. He felt awkward talking about money matters and politely ended the conversation.

Since then, in my drives around the city, I've seen the sign for Salvation's Nest. But each time it's in a different storefront, in a differ-ent strip mall. I've even seen those vehicles parked out front. I guess that building fund for a permanent new church is still a bit short.

I never did know what their minimum charge for an angel was, but I hope Libby has plenty of them now, surrounding her in heaven.

Caring Comments

+ It's not the caregiver's place to make judgments about someone's religious beliefs, of course. But Libby was in the middle stages of Alzheimer's or dementia; I felt I had to protect her. She told me she had been going to that church and those preachers for years, presumably long before her mind began to slip. She had certainly given them money then—rationally, freely—long before I came into her life. And she certainly had the right to continue to do so as long as they weren't taking advantage of her vulnerable mental state. Yet I wonder if they had any idea who the little old lady was who gave them all that money. I doubt it.

+ Religion, church and spirituality can be especially important in the difficult existence of an Alzheimer's patient. Some researchers theorize that religion may even slow the disease's progression, but it's a claim difficult to test and prove.

In 2005 the Web site of Science and Theology News reported that Canadian and Israeli researchers found that religious practice did, in fact, slow the progress of Alzheimer's disease. Dr. Yakir Kaufman, director of neurology at Sarah Herzog Memorial Hospital in Jerusalem, authored the study, which was presented at the American Academy of Neurology's 2005 annual meeting.

"We learned that Alzheimer's patients with higher levels of spirituality or higher levels of religiosity may have a significantly slower progression of cognitive decline," said Dr. Kaufman.

The researchers assessed 68 people between ages 49 and 94. The data revealed that higher levels of religiosity and private religious practices were significantly correlated with slower rates of cognitive decline.

But Dr. Andrew Newberg, a professor at the University of Pennsylvania, advises caution. Does spiritual activity slow Alzheimer's more effectively than other types of mental activity? "That's the $64,000 question," said Dr. Newberg, "whether or not the researchers can differentiate the positive effects of spirituality from other activities."

In other words, is the slowdown because the mental activity is spirituality or is it because spirituality is a form of mental activity?

+ The trust department of Libby's bank was always professional and protective of her privacy. Here is the base list of professional services bank trustees such as hers usually provide:

- Professional investment management
- Financial and estate planning assistance
- Complete record keeping
- Maintenance of cost-basis records for securities
- Collection of income from assets, receipt of stock dividends, exchanges, splits and other capital changes
- Comprehensive bill-paying service
- Receipt of non-asset related income such as social security benefits, pension payments and insurance annuity checks
- Medical claim processing
- Real estate services
- Payment of quarterly estimates for income tax
- Preparation of personal income tax returns
- Title holding of assets to assist estate planning
- Periodic accounting
- Execution of security trades

+ Despite the bank's fiduciary responsibility and its privacy policy, Libby maintained the right to leave her assets to whomever she pleased. With Libby and her reverends, I feared a scam, of course— a scheme to separate this wonderful woman (and everyone else in the church) from her money.

Scams targeting the elderly are everywhere. Some come in the mail, some come over the phone, some come disguised as the kindness of strangers.

+ I stressed to Libby the dangers of solicitations—by mail, phone or even at the door. I saw many brochures and envelopes from religious organizations around her home. I don't know if she gave to them or not. But I did see how willing she was at the church.

Was Libby scammed by her church and its leaders? No, probably not. Could she have been? Yes, easily.

Duty Bound

S ometimes in this business you're simply an observer. You may not work directly with particular clients, yet you cannot help noticing those who do. You watch them in action, and you're impressed.

Such was the case at the Alzheimer's care unit at Brighton Gardens. I went there regularly for a couple of years to be with my client Lenore, the remaining twin I introduced in an earlier chapter. The Brighton Gardens nurses were exceptional, every one of them. And like a natural athlete who makes it all look so easy, they performed their difficult tasks day in and day out, effortlessly, enthusiastically, smiles almost always on their faces.

It wasn't always easy for them to maintain their smiles. One reason was, for example, Dolly. She was a hard case, later-stage Alzheimer's. Her husband visited her nearly every day, but the lion's share of the caregiving was left to those nurses. And they earned every penny of their meager pay.

Dolly never stopped moving. She made her way up and down the halls, purse on her arm, on her way somewhere. She'd barge into Lenore's room and insist on escorting the two of us to lunch. When we'd get to the dining room, she'd say, "This isn't Caniglia's. I'll find out what's going on." And off she'd go to find out what had become of her favorite restaurant.

One time she pulled up alongside of me as I was walking toward the door and soon we were talking about children, even though I didn't

know if she had any of her own. I was going through some difficult times with my younger teenage son and opened a bit of my soul to Dolly. I told her about the disappearances, the petty crime, the truancy and the drugs. She nodded, patted my hand and offered me a tissue for my tears.

Then in the flash of an eye, she went blank, looked at me and asked in all sincerity, "Do you have children?"

"Yes, I do," I answered. "And I'm on my way to the principal's office right now."

It was the nurses who kept Dolly reined in, of course. They gave her the run of the place as long as she wasn't too much of a nuisance to other patients and as long as she never slipped past the combination-locked doors.

Many patients in Alzheimer's care facilities are far gone to the disease, of course. My own friends and family will sometimes comment to me how great I am for working with those far-gone folks. But my "skills" only go to a certain level. The truly great ones, the real health care heroes, are those professional nurses doing it so well day after day, night after night. Nerves of steel, hearts of gold.

Caring Comments

✦ My job as a care provider requires ongoing training in Alzheimer's care. I have passed basic courses and taken periodic refreshers. It's the pros, however—the nurses and social workers—who tirelessly keep up with the science of the disease and who must continually hone their care skills. The Dementia Care Professionals of America, a division of the Alzheimer's Foundation of America, is one organization that offers professional training and certification for the pros. The DCPA Web site, *www.careprofessionals.org*, gives an indication of the scope of the education and courses. The Alzheimer's Foundation site, *www.alzfdn.org*, is one of many excellent resources for caregivers, both professional and family. AFA's credo is simple but paramount: "No one should face this disease alone."

+ The need for Alzheimer's caregivers, professional or family/friend, is likely to skyrocket, if the 2007 statistics and projections from the Alzheimer's Association turn out to be anywhere close to accurate. A few of the frightening numbers:

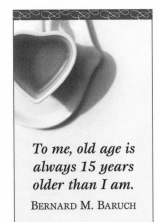

- In 2007 there were more than 5 million people in the United States with the disease.

To me, old age is always 15 years older than I am.

BERNARD M. BARUCH

- That number could increase to 7.7 million by 2030 and soar to 16 million by 2050.

- Someone in America develops Alzheimer's every 72 seconds.

Without a cure or effective delaying treatments, someone in America will develop Alzheimer's every 33 seconds by 2050.

Choosing an Eldercare Home

Brighton Gardens is clearly an excellent facility, the ideal home for Dolly. But how can a family member or friend know if a nursing home will be excellent?

Placing a loved one in a nursing home can be difficult. Families always struggle with making the "right choice" and feel guilty about the process. Make sure your loved one has been appropriately evaluated in determining the level of service he or she will require in a nursing home or assisted living facility.

Then visit possible choices. Many senior care organizations offer suggestions for choosing the right home. On the next page you'll find a simple checklist based on those suggestions.

Facility checklist

Observations to make:

+ Appearance of building and grounds
+ Overall cleanliness
+ Smell
+ Staff attitudes and helpfulness
+ Taste, smell and look of the food (stay for a meal)
+ Resident behavior
+ Resident appearance
+ Room size and furnishings

Questions to ask:

+ Do residents determine their daily routines, including bedtimes?

+ Is there a council of residents or family members? When does it meet?

+ Are state inspection reports available?

+ What is the staff-to-resident ratio?

+ How long do nurses and nurse assistants spend with each resident in the course of a normal day?

+ Does the home use any nursing agency staff?

+ Is staff turnover high?

I advise my clients to observe the facility's receptionist/front desk staff. That person is the frontline of the frontline staff. She or he can set the tone and affect the mood of the entire facility. Is she or he friendly? Knowledgeable? Helpful to visitors? Concerned about residents? Interact well with staff? A top person at the front desk doesn't guarantee a facility's quality, but a less-than-stellar person could be an indicator of problems.

Also, learn as much as you can about the facility's entertainment and activities programs. And observe them in action. Watch the entertainment/activities director; notice how the patients react to him or her. Again, mood, tone and spirit are essential to the mission of a nursing home.

Not surprising, Dolly's Brighton Gardens home employed wonderful front-desk and activities personnel. In fact, the entire staff was always professional, never "faking" their concern and compassion. They cared, and it showed.

Never Enough Stuff

Our first trip to the supermarket:

1 case tomato soup
1 case kidney beans
1 case frozen orange juice
12 half gallons ice cream
27 packages Lil' Miss brownies
30 Banquet frozen dinners
6 bottles V-8
7 jars Alfredo sauce

I got it all to the car, loaded up the trunk and back seat, helped Beverly into the passenger's seat and drove slowly to her house. Then I did it in reverse: helped her out of the car, unpacked the trunk and backseat and then began hauling all of the boxes and bags into her two-bedroom, one-story house.

I hadn't gotten a good look inside when I picked her up; we were too busy introducing ourselves to each other. Our first stop was the bank to cash her monthly Social Security check and then on to the market to spend a goodly chunk of it.

Now as I carried case after case, bag after bag into the house, I couldn't mask my amazement. Every nook and cranny, every square inch and square foot was packed with *stuff*: food, clothes, books, magazines, toys, racks, boxes, piles, stacks. Floor to ceiling, wall to wall. A narrow path had been cleared from the front door through the living room and on into the crowded kitchen.

My eyes couldn't take it all in, and my aching arms looked for someplace—anyplace—to set down the boxes and bags. She sat herself down in the only piece of living room furniture—a small chair in the middle of the path—and barked out suggestions:

"On top of that dress rack."

"Slide it under that end table."

She was in her early 80s, weathered face, scraggly long gray hair falling from beneath a baseball cap on her head. No teeth. She looked like an old Willie Nelson, an old *female* Willie Nelson. The commands continued:

"Not there, over there."

"On top of the magazines."

"Just stack it in front of that TV."

That TV was a giant, 50-something-inch screen almost buried in the midst of everything else. As I slid one box onto another, both of them in front of the TV screen, I asked, "But how are you going to watch television with all of this in the way?"

She smiled a toothless smile. "That's okay. I've never even turned it on. I bought it on a whim."

It was more than a whim, of course, that compelled Beverly to purchase that TV. And the 43 Cabbage Patch dolls, still in their boxes, stacked to the ceiling, all connected by spider webs. And the Elvis Presley fan magazines and dolls. And the scores of hats, many similar in style but different in color. Racks of clothes, a price tag still dangling from each piece. Stacks of Corning Ware casserole dishes. Endless Tupperware, never used. Two exercise bikes ("The only exercise I ever got was back when I'd push my shopping cart up and down the aisles of the liquor store to replenish my booze supply"), chairs stacked vertically to the ceiling. And the ceiling itself dripping with more spider webs that hung down into the stuff and seemed to keep it all from falling in on itself. And on Beverly, a queen in her cluttered castle as she sat on her pathway throne.

She was an obsessive compulsive. A hoarder, a shopaholic.

"Maybe you should get rid of some of these empty cardboard boxes," I said, seeing them sprinkled about everywhere and assuming they were of no use.

"No!" she said brusquely. "What if I need one someday."

I spent quite awhile in the kitchen, rearranging things in the freezer compartment of her refrigerator so I could stash away all of that ice cream. She could hear my struggle. "You know, they took away my booze and my sex," she called out from her chair in the path. "But they can't take away my ice cream."

After I'd finally gotten everything put away, tucked away and piled away, we chatted. She sat; I stood—in the path.

She asked me my birthday (March 10).

"Oh, no, you're a Pisces!" She seemed genuinely dismayed. "We'll never get along! I'm an Aries. That's a bad combination. George, my boyfriend for 14 years, was another goddamn Pisces, and he was as lazy as the day is long. Always drunk."

"Well, I've been married to an Aries for 36 years," I said. "And we seem to get along."

She smiled, got up and made her way down the path and into the kitchen. I could hear her digging around. After a few minutes, she returned to the living room and handed me two coffee cups, one decorated with Pisces the fish, the other with Aries the ram.

"Thank you, but you don't have to . . ."

"No big deal. I've got plenty more. I saw them in a store in Florida and bought 'em all."

We both smiled. It was the beginning of a beautiful friendship.

Our routine was monthly at first. When her Social Security check arrived, on the 4th or 5th of the month, she called my agency and arranged for my services.

We'd start out with a trip to the bank to cash the check and then visit several stores, buying new food and merchandise, sometimes returning the old. In fact, I can remember almost as many trips hauling stuff *into* the stores as I can hauling stuff *out*. For example, there were the six unassembled coat racks we brought back to Menards, a home improvement store, and the 14 purses to Kohl's Department Store, and the 10 purses to Burlington Coat Factory (where we bought six more), and the seven hats to Younker's Department Store, and the five hats to Kohl's (where we bought three more) and the memorable day when she tried to return 16 hats to the Goodwill, even though she knew the store had a no-returns policy.

"I just did it to have a good argument," she said, as we carried the hats back to the car.

Ah, the Goodwill. I'm a bit of a scavenger myself; I love a great thrift shop. But a trip to a Goodwill store with Beverly was a nightmare. I'd follow her around the larger Goodwill facilities with a chair I'd find up front that was light enough to carry. She'd collapse into it every few yards when she was too tired to lean on the shopping cart anymore.

During one adventure, she was on the hunt for a one-piece angel food cake pan. It was the only type suitable for her meatloaf specialty. "You mix up anything you want in the meatloaf," she explained as we sought out the kitchen wares, "form it into the angel food cake pan and bake it. You spray plenty of Crisco into it first because you gotta be able to dump the meatloaf out of the pan and onto a big platter. Then you take your mashed potatoes and fill the center hole in the meat and sprinkle the whole thing with cheese."

I have tried it—several times, in fact. It's a great conversation piece.

We didn't find the correct pan on that trip, but she did manage to buy about a dozen lids for saucepans.

"Why all these lids?" I asked.

"Well, I know I've got the pans for 'em at home," she said. "C'mon, let's go try on hats."

As we made our way toward women's wear, I took a stand. "I'm not trying on old, rotten used hats in a Goodwill," I said. She was taken aback, and maybe a little hurt.

"Well, my house is much dirtier than this and you go in there."

Now I was a bit taken aback. "You got me there," I said. "But I'm still not trying on any hats."

She did, of course. Tried on nine of them, one after the other, giving me a look each time. She put them all in the cart.

On our way back toward the front of the store, I noticed two African statues, a man and a woman. They were priced separately, which was fine with me because I really liked the woman and not the man. I picked her up and put her in the cart.

"What about the man?" Beverly asked.

"The man is ugly," I said. "I'm not getting him. They're priced separately."

"You can't do that! You'll break up the pair!" She was getting agitated.

"I can too," I said. "They're priced that way."

She stood there and just looked at me. I stood my ground.

"I'm not getting the man. It'll be my problem, not yours. They are priced separately."

She didn't say another word to me. We proceeded to the checkout, where I bought the lady statue. While I was doing so, she went and put all of the pan lids back on the shelf.

She didn't say another word until the Wendy's drive-thru where she struck up an argument with the teenage cashier about the recently raised price on the chicken nuggets. When we returned to her house, she didn't invite me to stay and chat.

Sometimes during our travels we'd run into neighborhood acquaintances, and the conversations were never boring. "I thought

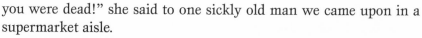
you were dead!" she said to one sickly old man we came upon in a supermarket aisle.

"No," he said, "but damn near. Lost more than a hundred pounds. Looks like you did too."

She had. One hundred and forty pounds, to be exact. And the skinny old man had known her in her bloated, boozing days with boyfriend George. We continued slowly on our way up the aisle; the old man shuffled off in the opposite direction. But the meeting had her thinking about George.

"When he died, I cried and cried," she said softly. "And that's when I picked up this buy-everything-that's-not-nailed-down habit. It used to be just garage sales, but when he conked, I started in on department stores. He'd have killed me if he knew what I've spent."

"See, you did love him in your own way," I said, trying to be supportive.

But her pensive moment was finished: "Nah, I just needed to have someone to argue with. I miss him."

One of our day trips took us out on the Interstate highway to an antique mall to check out collector glassware. And chairs. And anything and everything else. As we walked inside, she was weak and a bit wobbly but wouldn't let me hold her arm. "I don't want to be dependent on no one," she snapped.

I can be stubborn too. I insisted she let me push her around in one of the store's wheelchairs, or we'd turn around and go right back to the car. She grumbled and plopped down into the chair.

The building was huge, the size of an airplane hangar. We rolled up and down every aisle, perused every booth and case. Every time she came across Pepsi collector glasses decorated with Looney Tunes characters, she'd tell me to take them up to the counter.

"I can't make up my mind which ones I want," she said. "So let's line 'em up, then I can decide."

"But I know you have seven or eight Tweety Birds at home," I protested. "And I've seen way too many Yosemite Sams. These look just the same to me."

"Oh, but they're not," she insisted. "I know they're not."

So three hours later there were rows and rows of cartoon Pepsi glasses lined up on the counter, ready for her inspection. I'd also dragged a set of four kitchen chairs up to the front for her. They'd been marked down from $250 to $79—too good a deal to pass up. I tried to imagine how they could possibly be crammed into her overflowing house.

The clerks at the front desk were not at all pleased. Not only were the glasses monopolizing their counter space, now she demanded they group them and line them up by character. There were at least 80 or 90 glasses.

Then came the hard part, the agony of making a decision. I tried to talk her out of the chairs, while she pondered the Tweetys, Sylvesters and Sams. She didn't appreciate the distraction and simply said: "The chairs are marked down from $250. Put them in the car."

I was too exhausted to argue, so I dutifully hauled them outside and figured out a way to cram them into the car.

When I returned, she was still agonizing. The Tasmanian Devil was a sure thing—it's rare and a bargain at $12. She kept moving other glasses around on the counter like they were pieces in some kind of cartoon chess game. The clerks did not appreciate the game; they stood sullen and silent.

She looked up at me. "This Porky Pig has a different skin color from Petunia."

"He sure does," I answered. "Does that mean they can't be a set? The Porky seems much older than Petunia. Is he more valuable?"

She looked past me, pondering the imponderable. She was in her zone, her buyer's trance, another level. I remained silent.

It was another hour before the glasses were rejected, selected, wrapped and paid for: $250 worth.

After handing over the money to the exhausted but relieved clerks, she turned to me and said, "Do you think I really need those chairs?"

My look was my answer.

"Oh, I guess I can't *not* buy them for $79."

Our routine together grew slowly beyond the once-a-month Social Security sprees. Sometimes we stopped for chicken nuggets and she'd take them home. I offered to buy her a sit-down dinner somewhere to celebrate her birthday, but she wanted nothing to do with it. "I ain't got no choppers," she explained. "I ain't eatin' in a restaurant."

Other times we'd simply sit and talk at her house. Well, she'd sit and I'd stand or lean on a box. She'd tell me stories from her hard life of heavy drinking, smoking and partying ("Boy, could I slam down the booze."). She mentioned her two children: a doctor son who rarely contacted her and a gay daughter whom she talked about proudly.

She was apprehensive about her daughter's upcoming wedding, but not because she disapproved on moral grounds. Instead, she was concerned because her daughter's fiancé was so much younger. I told her it would work out just fine since the two of them had already been together for four or five years. But Beverly claimed you could never trust a younger spouse. "I wonder which one is the man," she mused.

Mostly she didn't say much about her family, however, and our sessions together continued to be predictably unpredictable.

On one visit to her house, I noticed tall, thick weeds growing outside her front door and offered to cut them for her. Did she have anything I could use to get the job done?

"Well, there's a small Sears Craftsman hedge clipper in a box underneath the bed, near the foot end, about in the middle." I made my way into the bedroom, past the stacks and piles to the foot of the bed. I knelt down, reached under tentatively and felt around for a box. There were several, along with bags and loose items I couldn't identify with just my fingers.

"Find it?" she called out from her living room throne. "I bought those clippers in 1983 but I've never used 'em."

I slid a box out from underneath: Craftsman. "I got 'em."

"Good," she said. "There's probably still a price tag on the box. I think I paid $9.95."

There was a tag: $9.95.

I trimmed the weeds down to their thick roots, cleaned off the blades, put the clipper back in the box and slipped the box back into its assigned place beneath the bed.

Another day—an important one in our friendship as it turned out—she had three boxes of her clothes sorted out for me when I arrived. "You remind me so much of me when I was younger," she said. "We're cut from the same cloth. These things will look great on you."

Virtually all of it, price tags still attached, was from the late 1970s and early 1980s. Not exactly my style. About the only things I'd ever seen that I might actually want were a couple of vintage leopard jackets and leopard handbags hanging deep in a hall closet.

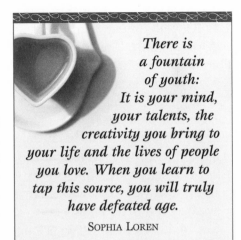

There is a fountain of youth: It is your mind, your talents, the creativity you bring to your life and the lives of people you love. When you learn to tap this source, you will truly have defeated age.

SOPHIA LOREN

"I don't need any of your stuff," I tried to explain. "I've got plenty of my own at home." But she insisted and before I knew it, I was loading it into my car.

Later that afternoon I phoned my agency and told them about the "gifts"; the next day I stopped by to get her to sign an agency form. She signed, but gave me even more. She said she had never given anything to anybody but me—because we both have the same taste.

Soon I had eight boxes of stuff that I had my husband stash in a corner of the basement. But every time I saw her, she asked about the clothes, in detail. What had I tried on? Did I like this piece, or that one? Did my Aries husband like them?

I finessed the questions as best I could, but one day decided to show up wearing a pair of her black stirrup stretch pants. She recognized them immediately and was thrilled. "I thank my lucky constellations for sending me you!"

But then when no other pieces appeared on my body and I continued dodging her pointed questions, she began asking for things back, one item at a time: the white turtleneck, the blouse with the tiny pink flowers, and on it went. She remembered each and every one of them. And I returned them as requested.

Finally one day she blurted out, "You've only worn one pair of pants that I gave you. Why don't you just bring it all back!"

I said I would, of course, but suggested I donate some of it to a women's shelter. She wouldn't hear of it and wanted everything back.

As I schlepped in the eight boxes during my next visit and struggled to find a place to put them, she simply sat silent in her chair, looking puzzled and hurt. Finally, she said softly, "I guess you just didn't need all those clothes."

My eyes began to well with tears and my voice cracked as I said, "Beverly, I tried to tell you that, every time. But you just didn't listen."

Uncomfortable silence for a few long seconds, then she said, "I've seen a lot of psychiatrists in my day—too many, in fact—so I'm going to use a little of their jargon for this situation. I did hear you say you didn't need any of the things I wanted to give you, but I didn't want to listen. I so wanted to project myself and my daughter onto you. I so wanted you to be…"

She couldn't finish. Again, a long silence. Finally, she reached into a nearby box, pulled out a garish red sweater, held it up, winked at me and said, "C'mon, how can you *not* want this?"

We both laughed, with tears in our eyes.

And then went shopping, this time to a health food store. Once again the experience was stressful. After much deliberation and aisle-roaming, she bought several high-end vitamins—by the case. She proceeded to argue with the clerk about a 20 percent price discount that was being offered on some bargain brands. She wanted the same deal—and she (eventually) got it.

On the way home, she asked me to stop at a drug store so she could get the latest copy of the *National Enquirer*, her favorite source for news. We went to a Walgreen's. It was a hot day so I told her I'd leave the car running along with the air conditioning while I went in to get an *Enquirer*. "I'll lock you in so you don't get carjacked."

"Carjacked?" she said. "Maybe they'll rape me!"

"Don't get your hopes up," I said. We both laughed, and I kept laughing all the way into the store, nearly wetting my pants. I picked up the *National Enquirer* from exactly where she said it would be.

Later that month we went to a Toys R Us to check out the newly redesigned Cabbage Patch dolls. She was unimpressed with the new line, and soon the doll department manager had joined us and all three of us were complaining about the new look. Beverly was getting tired and wobbly during the conversation, so I rounded up a toy chair for her to plop down into. Which she did. The queen in her toy court.

The manager, of course, tried to interest her in other dolls, but surprisingly Beverly wasn't buying. "I don't want to get hooked on another cute doll," she said. "And besides, my knees are killing me."

The manager, still hopeful of a sale of some kind, told us about a friend who recently had double knee replacement surgery at the ripe old age of 105.

Beverly nearly fell off her tiny chair. "Where's that doctor?" she asked. "Mine keeps telling me I'm too old for help."

"Montana," said our new friend, but Beverly was not discouraged.

"Oh, Colleen," she said. "We're gonna find us a new doctor. There's gotta be one in Nebraska."

And thus began our newest shopping spree: in the medical field.

Her health was not good. The knees. The back. The teeth. The bipolar. The epilepsy. The intestinal problems. Not to mention the obsessive compulsive disorder. Over the course of just a few weeks we visited eight doctors. While they all agreed that she needed help, primarily back surgery, none of them seemed eager to don the scrubs and have at her. She was too old and infirm; the surgery would be too risky.

So they delayed or referred her to one specialist or another. Luckily, she had good health insurance, so she was persistent. Finally, she got what she wanted: scheduled surgery. But then there was yet another delay. The surgeon recommended she see a psychiatrist first, apparently because she was bipolar and she took no medication to control it.

"What a goddamned crock," she said. "Now they think I'm too crazy to have surgery. I'll just give him a piece of my mind."

"I wouldn't do that," I said.

But that's how the psychiatric interview began: tense, confrontational, argumentative. Once again, a reflection of Beverly's personality. But as I had seen so many times with so many clerks at so many checkout counters, this difficult old woman could quickly become a charmer and win people over.

Sometime during the session, the psychiatrist asked her to write a complete sentence, apparently to see if she knew what one was. She did, of course, and surprised the doctor with this simple, complete one: "Let's be friends."

The two of them were soon getting along splendidly, and by session's end he had okayed her for the back surgery—some kind of spinal clean out. I never did understand what it was; she didn't confide everything in me.

I took her to the hospital for the operation and stayed with her right up until they wheeled her away for prep.

I visited her in the hospital the day after she'd gone under the knife. She was propped up in bed, wearing one of her many Elvis baseball caps. As the nurse on duty left the room, Beverly nodded after her and said to me, "That one's okay. She told me I look like Willie Nelson. And I do." She smiled that toothless grin.

She was anxious to get home, of course, and argued to be released as soon as possible—way too soon in my non-medical opinion. I told her so when I dropped her off at home. "I'll be fine," she said.

But that night she called me and said, "Maybe I should have stayed in the hospital." The pain was getting to her, and she was having renewed intestinal problems.

"Should I come over and help?" I asked.

"No, I made it to the bedroom and I'll just stay put."

I checked on her every day for the rest of that week, and she gradually got better. By the following Monday we were in her bank, where she proceeded to cause quite a scene in a dispute with a new teller. The young girl behind the counter insisted that Beverly show ID to get $50 cash back when she deposited her Social Security check. Annoyed, Beverly pulled a weathered state ID card from her purse. "I've been banking here for 30 years and no one has ever hassled me like this before."

The ID had expired 10 years earlier. The stubborn new clerk wouldn't accept it, and Beverly was outraged. The manager got involved. The customers behind her in line got involved. I got involved: "It's got her picture on it!" I said in frustration. "It's her. So what if it's expired!"

We lost the battle, but she was in fighting form again. We retreated to the car and proceeded to Menards, where we returned four cans of spray paint.

The fighting form didn't last. The intestinal churning was so severe she didn't dare leave her house, even to shop. She sent me out to buy peach yogurt for her. She handed me a $20 bill and said, "You're the only person I've ever trusted to shop for me."

I accomplished the mission, but not without a little stress of my own. The first store was out of peach yogurt but, thankfully, the second wasn't.

February turned into March, and after the first few days of the month I still hadn't gotten a call from her to make our regular check-cashing run. Even my agency was concerned—she hadn't called to schedule her days with me for the rest of the month. The agency sent someone over to the house, but Beverly was not there. A neighbor said there had been an emergency a few nights before and an ambulance had come.

I immediately called her favorite hospital and located her, in the critical care unit. I hurried to visit her and was apprehensive when I had to don a paper gown and latex gloves before going into her room.

She looked at me weakly, smiled toothlessly and said: "You'd have loved it. The paramedics had to use a sling to get me out of the house. They couldn't get their gurney through to me."

Apparently the intestinal problems had been exacerbated by the many antibiotics she'd been prescribed and encouraged to take. Now the situation was serious.

I told Beverly I would check on her house and pick up the mail (including the Social Security check). As she drifted into sleep, the nurse came back in and said to me, "You're the first person we've seen or heard from. Does she have family?"

"Yes," I answered.

"Are they estranged?" asked the nurse.

"Well," I said, "they live out of town but she talks about her daughter a lot and I think they're friendly."

"We are," mumbled Beverly from her half-sleep.

"Should I call her?" I asked.

She nodded. I called her daughter in Florida that evening and filled her in on the situation.

The next day at the hospital, her daughter was there, also dressed in paper gown and latex gloves. Beverly was lucid and calm and proudly introduced Patty to me. The three of us looked at some of

Patty's recent wedding pictures for a while, but I felt a bit out of place so I excused myself and slipped away.

That weekend my husband and I were taking a trip to Phoenix with friends. Before we left, I dropped off Beverly's mail at the hospital and chatted with her until she faded into sleep. Outside the room, Patty told me that the situation seemed to be getting worse not better.

We came home from Phoenix on March 11th. I called Patty's cell phone number to check on Beverly. She had died the day before, March 10th, my birthday.

An Aries and a Pisces, still connected.

Postscript

Patty and her life partner spent a couple of weeks handling Beverly's affairs. They arranged for her burial in Iowa, in a plot next to her father and mother. They scheduled a weekend "estate sale" at the house, but allowed the Nebraska Food Bank charity in first to take all of the foodstuff in all of the cupboards, drawers and crannies.

Patty and partner organized as much of the rest of it as they could. They found a box with about $1,000 in cash and a huge purse with every receipt for every item ever bought, organized by date and store.

The night before the sale, Patty called and asked if there was anything I wanted. "Well, maybe some of that fun, funky leopard stuff she has—the jackets and the purses."

The next day we joined the stream of bargain hunters, professional yard-salers and eBay entrepreneurs to see what it all looked like, now sort of organized and spread out on the lawn as well as everywhere inside. The single narrow path through the living room had been replaced by a variety of paths between and among all of the boxes, racks and stacks.

I didn't want to stay long and watch all those people paw through everything. So when Patty handed me that leopard stuff, I gave her a hug and said goodbye. She thanked me for being such a good friend to her mom.

The leopard jackets and handbags are part of my wardrobe now. They're fun to wear and use, and they'll always remind me of her.

But I keep expecting her to call and say she wants them back.

Caring Comments

+ Without a doubt, Beverly was the most unusual client/lady/friend I've ever encountered. She was exhausting; she was exhilarating. She was overwhelming; she was fun and funky. She never did reveal too much of her life story to me, but the few nuggets she did drop in made me think it had been a rather turbulent four-score-and-then-some. I always make sure I focus on the clients and allow them to share as little or as much as they please. It's their lives they're interested in, not mine.

I'm pleased that I was able to fill the role of diplomat for Beverly. At the stores, restaurants, bank and doctors' offices, I helped smooth over the tense situations and keep the confrontations from escalating. Beverly's social graces had eroded, due to stubbornness and insecurity. It's a common reaction to the uncertainties of aging. Caregivers often find themselves mediating, explaining and defusing, and must keep their cool when the situation is getting hot. It's rarely easy, but it's part of the job.

+ Often the most difficult challenge facing a caregiver from outside a family is to pick up on and react to the dynamics within that family. The caregiver must be attuned to those tensions and stresses every family has and—at a minimum—not compound them. Even better, look for ways and situations that will ease things and bring a few smiles into the family's hard time. Be a catalyst for calmness, not conflict. I'm glad I called Patty.

+ I have since discovered that even though compulsive shopping is smiled upon by our materialistic society, it is far from funny. Stanford Professor Lorrin Koran, who wrote about the disorder in the *Journal of Clinical Psychiatry*, says it best in an online article about his study: "Compulsive shopping leads to serious psychological, financial and family problems including depression, overwhelming debt and the breakup of relationships. People don't realize the extent of damage it does to the sufferer."

Compulsive shopping can be treated by therapy and, in some cases, with prescription drugs. It can be weakened and controlled. As a caregiver, I didn't do much to help Beverly control her compulsion. I'd usually give it a try at the beginning of a spree. I'd say something like, "Listen, you don't want to buy all this stuff and then have buyer's remorse tomorrow. You know we'll just end up taking a lot of it back." She'd then give me a look that would shut me up every time. She was in her zone, her trance. The next thing I knew, I was busy keeping up, carrying chairs, hauling merchandise, smoothing things over—but never trying on hats at the Goodwill.

+ Hoarding may go hand-in-hand with compulsive shopping, but hoarding itself can be its own problem. Sometimes people hoard stuff. Sometimes they hoard cats or other animals. Who hasn't heard about the crazy old lady with 56 cats in her home that was raided by the local animal control authorities? A fact sheet published by the Los Angeles County Department of Mental Health lists these reasons why people, primarily seniors, hoard:

- Items are perceived as valuable
- Items provide a source of security
- Fear of forgetting or losing items
- Constant need to collect and keep things
- Obtaining love not found from people
- Fear others will obtain their personal information
- Physical limitations and frailty
- Inability to organize
- Self neglect
- Stressful life events

Treating this obsessive compulsive disorder is anything but simple. An intervention will work only with at least some acceptance by the hoarder. Professionals, as well as family members, should participate. The ultimate goal is to convince and encourage the hoarder to slowly and steadily consider each of the many possessions in new item-specific ways as something:

- to be thrown away;
- to be recycled;
- to be given away;
- or to be kept and put away.

The choices seem easy and routine, but to the hoarder they can be an almost insurmountable challenge. One thing certain about hoarding or any other obsessive compulsive disorder: The effects are serious; treatment is difficult.

✦ Although I was frustrated that I couldn't have been more helpful to Beverly as she sought medical advice and medical relief from her physical infirmities, I also knew that privacy laws and regulations always prevail. Even if I wanted to get more involved—interviewing doctors, questioning prognoses—I could not. All of that was Beverly's private information and her choice whether to share it with me. She shared very little. To get an indication of the labyrinthine world of medical privacy rights, take a look at the U.S. Department of Heath & Human Services Office of Civil Rights Web site, *www.hhs.gov/ocr/hipaa*. You'll get a better understanding of the need for privacy and the privacy challenges caregivers face.

Caring Resources

The powerful message cannot be repeated enough: You are not alone. The agencies, associations and companies included here are excellent starting points in your search for just the right information or assistance for you or someone you love.

We've listed helpful, credible Web sites, including phone numbers where available for those of you without Internet access.

AARP
(888) 687-2277 + *www.aarp.org*

AARP is a treasure trove of advice, assistance and peace of mind for anyone over 50, especially caregivers. Its Web site includes a valuable Family, Home & Legal section with answers to just about any caregiving concern—from driving and home design to hospice and grief. From the site you can link to *AARP The Magazine*, the association's bi-monthly membership publication, and *AARP Bulletin*, its useful, senior-issues tabloid.

Administration on Aging
(202) 619-0724 + *www.aoa.gov*

The AOA is under the administrative umbrella of the U.S. Department of Health and Human Services. Its Web site provides a comprehensive overview of a wide variety of topics, programs and services related to aging. It is an excellent source for all things federal relating to eldercare and senior citizen issues. Helpful links connect you to other governmental agencies.

Alzheimer's Association
24-hour Alzheimer's help line: (800) 272-3900 ✦ *www.alz.org*

It's the world leader in Alzheimer research and support, the first and largest voluntary health organization dedicated to finding prevention methods, treatments and an eventual cure for Alzheimer's. If Alzheimer's has made its ugly way into your life and your family's life, you must familiarize yourself with this organization. Its Web site is packed with the latest news and research updates, as well as caregiving strategies and resources to deal with the disease.

Alzheimer's Champions
(800) 272-3900 ✦ *www.actionalz.org*

This Alzheimer's Association awareness and fundraising campaign hopes to recruit one person for every American with the disease—now more than 5 million. Celebrities have come on board and are prominent within the Champion's Web site, promoting Memory Walks, donations, lobbying, communication and other ways to get involved. The site's interactive "brain tour" uses simple, powerful graphics to show how the disease affects the brain.

Alzheimer's Foundation of America
(866) 232-8484 ✦ *www.alzfdn.org*

The AFA is a consortium of organizations—nonprofits, health-care facilities, government agencies, public safety departments and long-term-care communities—dedicated to aiding individuals with Alzheimer's disease and related illnesses, and their caregivers and families. Its Web site is a comprehensive source of information and help for caregivers. The CareCentral link offers an opportunity to create your own personal Web site to keep family and friends up-to-date on your caregiving challenges and successes.

American Medical Association
www.ama-assn.org

As you might expect, the AMA's mission is a broad one: "To promote the art and science of medicine and the betterment of public health." Although this Web site is primarily for the professionals, there are some gems for all of us. AMA DoctorFinder provides professional information about virtually every licensed physician in the United States and its possessions. There is also access to AMA reports and research.

American Red Cross
www.redcross.org

The organization's Web site is wide ranging, of course, and opens with the latest disaster news and Red Cross initiatives throughout the world. Within the site's Health and Safety Services section is an overview of the organization's Family Caregiving Program. The online store offers "Family Caregiving," a recently introduced reference guidebook and DVD, also available at Red Cross chapters.

American Society on Aging
(800) 537-9728 ✦ *www.asaging.org*

This is a professional organization, for "anyone who wants to stay on the cutting edge in the field of aging," including practitioners, educators, researchers, policymakers and service providers. Because it is a professional organization, its Web site is a no-nonsense source for the latest medical and legislative developments and easy access to a variety of pertinent publications.

Caregiver Media Group
(800) 829-2734 ✦ *www.caregiver.com*

This Florida-based organization has been providing information, support and guidance for family and professional caregivers since 1995. Its *Today's Caregiver* magazine was the first national publication dedicated to caregivers. Its comprehensive Web site includes information about its Fearless Caregiver Conferences, topic-specific newsletters, online discussion lists, chat rooms, resources and an online store.

Caregiver's Home
(203) 254-3538 ✦ *www.caregivershome.com*

This Web site is the online arm of the monthly newsletter *The Caregiver's Home Companion*. Its resource directory includes more than 40,000 entries—links to federal, state and local government sources and national associations. Its online archive has more than 2,500 articles on eldercare, caregiver resources, family caregiving, spousal caregiving and general health care. Online forums allow you to share insights and experiences with other caregivers anywhere.

Caring Connections
(800) 658-8898 ✦ *www.caringinfo.org*

This program of the National Hospice and Palliative Care Organization (NHPCO) is a national consumer initiative to improve care at the end of life. The initiative is supported by a grant from The Robert Wood Johnson Foundation. Caring Connections provides free resources and information to help people make decisions about end-of-life care and services *before* a crisis.

Dementia Care Professionals of America
www.careprofessionals.org

DCPA, a division of the Alzheimer's Foundation of America, offers membership, training, qualification and other benefits to health care professionals involved in dementia care. Even a quick perusal of the site gives an impressive, heartening look at the backgrounds, training and dedication of these important pros.

Eldercare Locator
(800) 677-1116 ✦ *www.eldercare.gov*

This public service of the U.S. Administration on Aging is the first step to finding resources for older adults in any U.S. community. Just one phone call or Web site visit provides an instant connection to resources that enable older people to live independently in their communities. The service links those who need assistance with state and local area agencies on aging and community-based organizations that serve older adults and their caregivers.

Family Caregiver Alliance
(800) 445-8106 ✦ *www.caregiver.org*

The FCA's National Center on Caregiving is a central source of information and technical assistance on caregiving and long-term care for policy makers, health and service providers, media, program developers, funding sources and families. The FCA site includes links to its publications, fact sheets, newsletters and research reports. Its Caregiver Tips page is a helpful and readable collection of advice from family caregivers as they deal with their own caring challenges. The Hot Topics page will link you to the latest caregiving articles and reports.

Family Caregiving 101
www.familycaregiving101.org

This initiative was created by two organizations profiled later in this list: the National Family Caregivers Association (NFCA) and the National Alliance for Caregiving (NAC). They combined their efforts and resources to focus specifically on family caregiving. The Family Caregiving Web site provides caregivers with the basic tools, skills and information they need to protect their own physical and mental health while they provide high quality care for their loved one.

FindLaw
www.findlaw.com

This Web site is a comprehensive resource for all things legal, including finding a lawyer in your area or having a lawyer contact you to help with your legal issues. The site also includes legal information on topics from traffic violations and auto accidents to real estate and bankruptcy. There's also the latest legal news, plus access to forms and contracts.

Home Instead Senior Care
(888) 484-5759 ✦ *www.homeinstead.com*

Based in Omaha, Neb., Home Instead is the world's largest provider of companionship and home care services for seniors. Franchise offices are located throughout the United States and in 10 other countries. Home Instead's services are designed for almost any living arrangement where an older adult simply needs human interaction and help with day-to-day activities.

Hospice Net
www.hospicenet.org

This Nashville-based nonprofit organization provides information and support to patients and familes facing life/threatening illnesses. The simple, user-friendly Web site answers questions, offers resources and provides inspiration—even as life is ending. The caregiver support articles are especially worthwhile. Helpful links give you online access to hospice organizations across the U.S. and beyond.

Legal Hotlines
www.legalhotlines.org

This Web site is sponsored by the AARP Foundation Technical Support for Legal Hotlines Project, which is supported by a grant from the U.S. Administration on Aging. The project provides technical assistance to legal hotline managers and developers. The Web site provides a compilation of hotline-related materials produced by the project as well as those produced by numerous other programs. Although the site is for those who work with legal hotlines, it is a quick source to find the hotlines and organizations in your area.

Mayo Clinic
www.mayoclinic.com

The famous Minnesota-based medical center has three main Web sites offering information, outlining services and summarizing research. The Health Information site, *www.mayoclinic.com*, includes updates on more than 35 diseases and lifestyle categories. The Medical Services site, *www.mayoclinic.org*, tells what's available at the clinic and how to access it. The Education and Research site, *www.mayo.edu*, looks at the latest in medical research and professional education.

Medicare Rights Center
Consumer Hotline (800) 333-4114 + *www.medicarerights.org*

The largest independent source of health care information and assistance in the U. S. for people with Medicare, MRC helps older adults and people with disabilities get good, affordable health care. Its Consumer Hotline provides direct assistance to older adults and people with disabilities, their friends, family, caregivers and professionals who have Medicare questions or problems. Hotline counselors respond to questions from individuals about available Medicare health plan options, rights and benefits.

MedlinePlus
www.medlineplus.gov

This federal government Web site, from the National Library of Medicine and the National Institutes of Health, is a valuable resource for virtually any health topic. MedlinePlus brings together authoritative information from government agencies and health-related organizations. It also includes extensive details about drugs, an illustrated medical encyclopedia, interactive patient tutorials and the latest health news.

MetLife Mature Market Institute

(203) 221-6580 ✦ *www.maturemarketinstitute.com*

The institute is MetLife's information and policy resource center on issues related to aging, retirement, long-term care and the 50 + marketplace. The institute has teamed up with the National Alliance for Caregiving and the National Association of Area Agencies on Aging to produce a valuable 38-page booklet called *Resources for Caregivers*. It can be downloaded from the site's What's New section or ordered by phone.

National Academy of Elder Law Attorneys

www.naela.org

This nonprofit association assists lawyers, bar organizations and others who work with older clients and their families. The NAELA offers information, education, networking and assistance to those who deal with the many specialized issues involved with legal services to the elderly and people with special needs. The site includes an easy-to-use search function to find an elder-law attorney near you.

National Alliance for Caregiving

www.caregiving.org

Established in 1996, the NAC is a nonprofit coalition of national organizations focusing on issues of family caregiving. Alliance members include grassroots organizations, professional associations, service organizations, disease-specific organizations, a government agency and corporations. The Alliance was created to conduct research, provide policy analysis, develop national programs and increase public awareness of family caregiving issues. Its Web site reports on those efforts and initiatives and includes caregiver tips and resources.

National Association of Area Agencies on Aging
(202) 872-0888 + *www.n4a.org*

It's the umbrella organization for the 655 area agencies on aging (AAAs) and more than 230 Title VI Native American aging programs in the U.S. The AAAs and Title VI programs provide services which make it possible for older individuals to remain in their homes, thereby preserving their independence and dignity. These home- and community-based services include information and referral, home-delivered and congregate meals, transportation, employment services, senior centers, adult day care and a long-term care ombudsman program.

National Association of Senior Move Managers
www.nasmm.com

NASMM is a nonprofit, professional association of organizations dedicated to helping older adults and their families with the physical and emotional aspects of moving. Its members are committed to maximizing the dignity and autonomy of older adults as they transition from one living environment to another. The Web site includes a locator map to find a senior moving service in your area.

National Center on Elder Abuse
www.elderabusecenter.org

NCEA is a national elder-rights resource for law enforcement and legal professionals, public policy leaders, researchers and the public. The center's mission is to promote understanding, knowledge sharing and action on elder abuse, neglect and exploitation. The site includes a section on Adult Protective Services, the state organizations whose caseworkers are the first responders to reports of abuse. Hotlines and helplines are listed.

National Family Caregivers Association
(800) 896-3650 ✦ *www.nfcacares.org*

The NFCA is an advocate for the more than 50 million Americans who care for loved ones with a chronic illness or disability or who are suffering the frailties of old age. Its Web site includes resources and information and also access to the NFCA Story Project, a collection of first-person accounts by family caregivers. Read their stories and maybe even submit your own.

National Institute on Aging
(800) 438-4380 ✦ *www.nia.nih.gov/Alzheimers*

The NIA's Alzheimer's Disease Education and Referral (ADEAR) Center was created in 1990 by the U.S. Congress to "compile, archive, and disseminate information concerning Alzheimer's disease for health professionals, people with Alzheimer's and their families, and the public." The NIA conducts and supports research about health issues for older people and is the primary federal agency for Alzheimer's disease research. Along with medical updates and legislative information, the Web site includes access to a variety of caregiving publications, most of them free.

National Women's Health Information Center
(800) 994-9662 ✦ *www.womenshealth.gov*

A division of the U.S. Department of Health and Human Services, Office on Women's Health, the center provides reliable information on women's health. Some 75 percent of caregivers are women, and many work outside the home. Included on the center's Web site is information on all major health concerns for women and prevention information for women.

Pets for the Elderly
(866) 849-3598 ✦ *www.petsfortheelderly.org*

PFE is a nonprofit organization that provides the gift of health and happiness to senior citizens in need, while saving the lives of dogs and cats. It makes donations to animal shelters throughout the United States that participate in a program for senior citizen adoption of a companion cat or dog. The Web site includes stories, research and ways to help.

Rosalynn Carter Institute for Caregiving (RCI)
www.rosalynncarter.org

The institute was established in 1987 on the campus of Georgia Southwestern State University (GSW) in Americus, Georgia, in honor of one of its most noted alumnae, former First Lady Rosalynn Carter. RCI works to establish local, state and national partnerships committed to building more effective long-term care systems and providing greater recognition and support for America's unsung heroes—the millions of caregivers, both family and professional.

Senior Days
www.seniordaysonline.com

At this Web site you can purchase additional copies of this book and, most important, you can link to the key Web sites we have listed here. Web addresses sometimes change, so by going to our Web site, you can be assured the links will be updated and more will be added. In addition, we encourage you to share your own tales from the frontlines of eldercare in our Caring Community section of the site.

Senior Drivers
www.seniordrivers.org

AAA's Foundation for Traffic Safety sponsors this helpful, comprehensive Web site. The four primary sections of the site are Driving Safely, with tips and guides to staying safe on the road; Giving Up Keys, for families and individuals when driving is no longer a viable alternative; Providers, for those who provide senior supplemental transportation systems; and Researchers, a look at current and past research addressing aging and mobility.

Strength for Caring
www.strengthforcaring.com

This award-winning Web site, sponsored by Johnson & Johnson Consumer Products Co., is an excellent source for caregiving information and assistance. The site is organized into six main sections: Caregiver Manual, Community, Health Conditions, Daily Care, Housing and Money & Insurance. The Caregiver Manual—loaded with tips, help and inspiration—is a must read. The comprehensive site is an online community as well as an online resource.

Tender Transitions
(800) 330-9567 ✦ *www.tendertransitions.net*

This senior relocation company services the Omaha and Lincoln metro areas of eastern Nebraska. Tender Transitions coordinates and implements all aspects of moving into new life situations. The owners and staff handle all the details to help smooth the process of transitioning from one residence to another.

Twinless Twins
(888) 205-8962 ✦ *www.twinlesstwins.org*

This organization offers support for twins and other multiples who have lost their twin due to death or estrangement at any age: "The unique aloneness we feel can best be understood by another twinless twin. You are not alone." The Web site includes a chat room and access to a brochure and a free e-newsletter.

U.S. Census Bureau
www.census.gov

Our country's leading source of data about ourselves, our society and our economy. The Web site is a treasure trove of facts and figures, including much information about our aging population. There are even population clocks that update the country's and world's populations every minute.

U.S. Department of
Health and Human Services
www.hhs.gov/ocr/hipaa

The Office on Civil Rights-HIPAA section of this giant federal Web site includes fact sheets, news, definitions and discussion concerning the privacy of personal health information and why and how it should be protected. HIPAA stands for the Health Insurance Portability and Accountability Act. Peruse the larger HHS site and find useful information on virtually any health topic, including aging.

Photo by: L.Randall Nogg

About the Authors

Colleen Nicol

Colleen Nicol has packed a lot of living into her 59 years. She's been a waitress, receptionist, retail clerk, real estate sales agent, entrepreneur, volunteer and, most recently, an in-home senior care companion. For the past 13 years, she has been employed by a highly regarded provider of non-medical care, assistance and companionship to the elderly. Nicol was the company's Alzheimer's Caregiver of the Year in 1997. Her formal education includes work toward an associate of arts degree from Honolulu Community College. She and her co-author husband, Brian, married for 39 years, have two sons, Kevin, 25, and Daniel, 23.

Brian Nicol

Brian Nicol's writing, editing and publishing career spans more than 30 years, most of them in Hawaii, Oregon and Nebraska. He was editor of *Honolulu Magazine*, the city and regional magazine of Hawaii, from 1982 until 1990. For a little more than two years, he was editorial director of Aster Publishing Corp. in Eugene, Oregon. Most recently, he was CEO of Home & Away Publishing, a AAA-owned media company that produces travel magazines with combined circulation of more than 5.5 million. Over the years, Nicol has been honored with numerous writing, editing and publishing awards. His book projects include work for Time-Life Books and Alouette Verlag of Germany. In his "spare" time, he writes screenplays; several of his scripts have won national awards.

I don't believe one grows older.
I think that what happens early on in life is that
at a certain age one stands still and stagnates.

T.S. ELIOT

✦

Forty is the old age of youth; fifty is the youth of old age.

VICTOR HUGO

✦

Age is a very high price to pay for maturity.

PAULO COELHO

✦

Middle age is when your age starts
to show around your middle.

BOB HOPE

✦

The older I grow the more I distrust
the familiar doctine that age brings wisdom.

H.L. Meneken

✦

Men and women approaching retirement age
should be recycled for public service work,
and their companies should foot the bill.
We can no longer afford to scrap-pile people.

Mahatma Gandhi

✦

If age imparted wisdom,
there wouldn't be any old fools.

Anonymous

✦

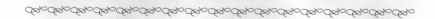

Index